VOICES of NAVAJO MOTHERS and DAUGHTERS
Portraits of Beauty

By Kathy Eckles Hooker
Photography by David Young-Wolff

Soulstice
PUBLISHING
books with *soul* • Flagstaff, AZ

Also by Kathy Eckles Hooker

Time Among the Navajo: Traditional Lifeways on the Reservation

Contents

Navajo Nation in blue, within the context of the Four Corners region of the United States

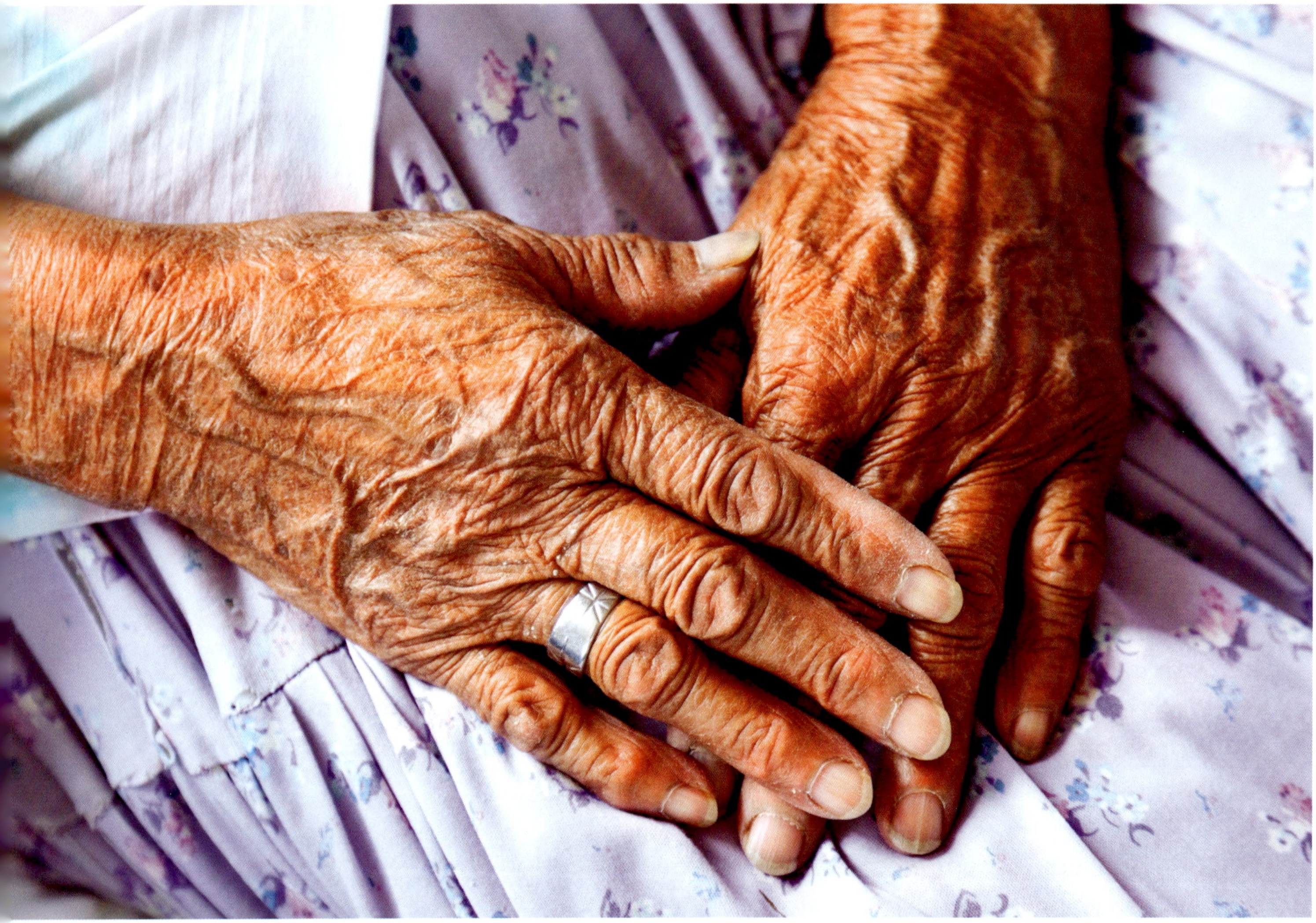

Hands of Nona Scott, Leupp, Arizona

Introduction

One Mother's Day morning, I read an article about the relationship between a Navajo mother and her daughter in my local newspaper in Flagstaff, Arizona, the *Arizona Daily Sun*. It brought back memories of the time my husband and I lived on the Navajo Reservation at Dilcon Boarding School more than thirty-five years ago. We both worked with Navajo children; he was their dentist, and I was their teacher.

The article sparked my interest, and I wondered how much had changed for Navajo women since my time at Dilcon. I knew of numerous anthropological studies of Navajos or Diné, meaning "The People," but I did not want interpretations. I wanted to hear the stories from the women themselves—to hear their voices. Was their culture still as strong as when I left in 1977? How might these changes have affected the roles of grandmothers, mothers, and daughters? Were the elders still passing stories and traditions to the next generation? What kind of lives did mothers wish for their daughters?

When I lived at Dilcon, I spent time with my students' families and witnessed the close bonds between parents and children. Moms and daughters wove rugs, picked Navajo tea, harvested ears of Indian corn, and cooked blood sausage. They worked side by side, occasionally quiet and other times chatting softly in Navajo. Watching them work and relate to each other inspired me. I wondered if this connection between mothers and daughters remained strong. I wanted to establish personal relationships with Navajo women, learn of their hopes, sorrows, and joys, and hear their touching life stories. This longing pulled me back to the reservation. The result is *Voices of Navajo Mothers and Daughters: Portraits of Beauty*—a collection of interviews and photographs of amazing, strong, and resilient Navajo women across generations.

Chapter 1, Women in Navajo Culture, introduces some of the cultural touchpoints that strongly affect the lives of many of the women we interviewed. Chapters 2 through 22 include the interviews with all twenty-one families. Because the interviews were conducted from 2009 to 2012, I recently reached out to each family again for updates on their lives in the intervening years. We have included all of the updated information we were able to collect. Chapter 23, The Impacts of History, provides the historical references that explain and connect everyday life in the Navajo Nation today with past traumas and experiences. The cultural and historical overview in Chapters 1 and 23 creates a context to allow for a deeper understanding of the women's stories.

> Watching them work and relate to each other inspired me. I wondered if this connection between mothers and daughters remained strong.

Raised in the eastern part of the United States, I knew little of the Navajo people when I moved to the reservation in 1975. I felt I had entered a foreign country because of unfamiliar language, dress, culture, and traditions. As an outsider and educator, I quickly became an eager student, wanting to absorb as much as possible about Diné history and culture.

My schooling began when I visited the camps of my pupils and spent time with their families. I witnessed much about the center of their society—the pivotal role of women.

I learned of the importance of sheep, vital to their culture and livelihood. Living and working in a boarding-school compound, I observed Navajo students in action and wanted to know how their schools came to exist. Scholars provided the history of The Long Walk and the imprisonment at Fort Sumner (see Chapter 23), which resulted in the establishment of schools and the Navajo-Hopi Land Dispute, all of which have had profound influence on the Navajos. Years later, the women's interviews in *Voices of Navajo Mothers and Daughters: Portraits of Beauty* validated these same influences.

The Interviews

To begin this project, I reached out to a few contacts in the hope that word would spread. I lived in Flagstaff, Arizona, near the Navajo Nation. As an English and social studies teacher in the Flagstaff Unified School District for more than thirty years, I had worked with Navajo teachers, administrators, instructional aides, and students.

Elaine Kasch, Director of Indian Education for the Flagstaff district, told me, "More Navajo students are enrolled in our district than on the Navajo Reservation." I was grateful when educators I knew began connecting me to Navajo grandmothers, mothers, and daughters. Through a friend, I discovered a Navajo weaver who worked in the deli of a local grocery store. A neighbor recommended a woman who sold merchandise in a Flagstaff shop. A local dentist mentioned the project during a conversation with a Navajo woman. Striking up conversations with Navajo daughters, mothers, and grandmothers in local restaurants led to even more interview subjects. Sharing the purpose of the project and sample photographs of Navajo women proved a powerful way of convincing others to participate. My most productive contact, Jim Kieffer, the former superintendent of Sanders Public Schools on the Navajo Reservation, recruited Navajo families who agreed to be interviewed and photographed.

Reactions to our interview requests were mixed. Many said yes and were eager to take part. Some said no because their mothers or grandmothers "felt shy or were too old." One great-grandmother, age 103, could not participate because it would "be too stressful." Another mother worried about the security of her children if their photos appeared in a book. In the end, my photographer, David Young-Wolff; his wife, Pam, who is also his assistant; and I completed a total of twenty-one interviews and photo shoots. All but a few of the mothers and daughters lived on the Navajo Nation, while the remainder lived in Flagstaff.

To cover significant aspects of the lives of mothers and daughters, I asked questions covering early childhood through adulthood:

Mothers

- Where were you born? If not in a hospital, describe your birth. Where was your daughter born?
- How did you feel when your daughter went to boarding school at age five or six?
- What traditions did you teach your daughter?
- Did you have an arranged marriage? If so, describe your first meeting with your husband-to-be and the ceremony.
- What kind of future do you wish for your daughter?
- How was your life different from your daughter's?
- What kind of work did your father and mother do?

Mothers and Daughters

- What kind of tasks did you do as a child?
- How did you feel when you went to school?
- Describe your boarding-school experience. What struggles and positive experiences did you have?
- How many brothers and sisters do you have?
- Tell me about a happy time.
- Tell me about a sad time.

- Describe a typical summer day and a typical winter day.
- Did you have a *kinaaldá* (puberty ceremony)? If so, would you describe it? (See Chapter 1 for more on the *kinaaldá*.)
- Do you weave? If so, who taught you?

Most of our initial meetings were with a mother or daughter; we met the rest of the family members at their ranches, called "camps," at the time of the interview and photography sessions. The interviews took place in one- or two-room houses where we sat on couches or outside using folding chairs. We followed the Navajo custom of having a "settling-in period," chatting informally and becoming comfortable before beginning the interviews. Once I asked the first question, the women seemed more relaxed. Many of the elders spoke Navajo exclusively, so their portion of the interview was translated by mothers, daughters, or granddaughters.

Being welcomed as guests, we understood the importance of showing respect when making personal inquiries. Some women wanted the questions ahead of time, so they felt comfortable when answering. I was heartened when one mother told us, "Nobody wants to know about us. They never come and talk to us about our lives. I am glad you came out to the reservation."

The Photographs

By David Young-Wolff

When Kathy asked me if I was interested in shooting photographs of Navajo mothers and their daughters, I immediately responded, "Yes!"

Photographers understand that there are many ways to approach a photo shoot. Having photographed subjects for more than forty-three years, I have developed a process that helps me determine my approach to each shoot. One of the most important aspects of this project was wanting the photos to portray reality: who the mothers and daughters really are, not who I might think they are. My objective was to have the viewer become engaged with the subject.

For the purpose in *Voices of Navajo Mothers and Daughters: Portraits of Beauty*, I wanted the audience to see how the mothers and daughters related to each other. When we first arrived at each location, I walked around, looking for places to shoot. This depended on both the available lighting and the importance of showcasing each family's environment. While Kathy interviewed the women, I sat and listened. Often I incorporated into the shoot what I learned. One instance was when a daughter talked about her mother's corral for the family's sheep and goats. The corral, made of pieces of wood, was fairly large. It remained in one spot for a long period of time until too much manure and dirt accumulated along the fence and inside the corral. It needed to be moved to a new and clean location. Her mom, a diminutive, elderly woman, was the one who physically moved the entire corral by herself. To connect the mother to the corral, we felt it important to photograph her near the structure. In another case, we learned that an abandoned building close by turned out to be a daughter's old preschool. We decided to shoot all their photographs there.

One challenge was communicating with the elders. In many situations, they lived in the same homes where their children had been born and raised. Their homes were isolated, and many spoke Navajo exclusively. Their daughters, speaking both Navajo and English, translated for their mothers. I do not speak Navajo, but my wish was to make the mothers feel comfortable when being photographed. My approach to photography has always been to treat people with the utmost respect. In this situation, I had to communicate my respect through my actions, not my words. If you honor people, they will eventually feel comfortable letting you enter their private lives.

Listening to the stories of generations of Navajo women and photographing their portraits has been an opportunity of a lifetime.

Editor's Note

We use the terms "Navajo" and "Diné" interchangeably and by preference of subject.

Navajo Stirring Sticks

Navajo women bind seven greasewood stems together to create their stirring sticks. Placed above doors and in kitchens, these bundles, also called "mush sticks," have several purposes.

In addition to being used in cooking and puberty ceremonies, the sticks hold a deeper meaning for Navajo families. Mothers view them as weapons against hunger, laziness, and poverty. The sticks must be washed with care and then oiled, using olive or grape-seed oil. When these are hung in a home, the family knows they will never go without food. Grandmothers pass their sticks down to the next generation. To a Navajo woman, stirring sticks complete a home and keep her family safe. (I adapted this information from a wonderful YouTube video called "A Diné Woman's Weapon Against Poverty and Hunger: Navajo/Diné Stirring Sticks/'Adeestsíín," by Navajo Grandma.)

The stirring stick symbol in this book was designed by Corey Begay. It is intended to honor Navajo women everywhere who share their stories and keep their families strong.

Generations of Navajo Hands, Flagstaff, Arizona

Chapter 1

Women in Navajo Culture

Navajos live within a matriarchal society. Unlike the women in male-dominated American or European cultures, the women of the Diné oversee the lives of The People. Native American filmmaker Billy Luther tells us, "Navajo women wear the trousers in the Navajo society. They work the land, they raise the kids, and they preserve the culture and traditions. And they butcher the sheep! So you see they are much more than just a pretty face!"[1] Traditionally, the Diné social order called for a newly married husband to reside with his wife and her family. The kinship is still matrilineal, following the female ancestral line.[2]

Changing Woman

The central role played by women in traditional Navajo cultures traces back to the Diné religion, in which *Asdzáá Naadleehi* (Changing Woman) is the spiritual mother and teacher of past and present Navajo women and creates a pathway for all Diné to follow. Changing Woman is the supreme holy deity, creating clans on the mother's side.[3]

Symbolizing the forces of the earth, Changing Woman aged by following the progression of the seasons: young in the spring when a new earth lives, growing through summer when the earth matures, elderly during the fall when the earth sheds its leaves, then dying in the winter, only to be reborn when spring returns.[4] Being Mother Earth, Changing Woman gave to the earth crops and livestock. Watching over them, she bestowed "reproduction, sustenance, and nurturance."[5]

Kinaaldá

As a spiritual being, Changing Woman matured into puberty in twelve days and experienced her first menstruation on that last day. The Holy People, ancestors of the Diné, created a unique and complex ceremony—the *kinaaldá*—to mark Changing Woman's coming of age. At the hands of the Holy People, she was "dressed in jewels [and] blessed with pollen from the dawn and from twilight, and with 'pollen' from many jewels and soft fabrics. . . . Her hair was bathed with dews and she was instructed to run toward the dawn. . . . She repeated this for four nights. On these days, when not involved in ceremonies, she occupied herself with planning the future of the Earth."[6]

Through the ages, young Diné women have celebrated this joyous observance of fertility to announce their entrance into womanhood with their new capacity to bear children.[7] Today the *kinaaldá* lasts four days and three nights, overseen by a close relative who reveals to the young woman the way to align herself with Changing Woman. In her book *Kinaaldá, A Study of the Navaho Girl's Puberty Ceremony,* Charlotte Johnson Frisbie states, "The *kinaaldá* is prophylactic, rather than curative; it ushers the girl into society, invokes positive blessings on her, insures her health, prosperity, and well-being, and protects her from potential misfortune."[8] Jaclyn Roessel, creator of the GrownUp Navajo company, writes that most young Diné women have one ceremony, but some have two. Changing Woman had four ceremonies because she had four periods. She kept two ceremonies for herself and offered two as gifts for future Navajo women. Having either one or two *kinaaldás* honors Changing Woman.[9]

As Margaret Marie Wauneka Goodwin conveyed, "My ceremony lasted four days. It was to honor the four seasons. I had to run every day. The first day I ran just a little ways. The next three days I had to run farther and farther. Running was to make me strong and have a healthy life. I wore a sash belt to help me with good posture. Each day I did a lot of grinding of corn, and that helped my fertility. I used the stones: the *metate* and *mano*. The third night and fourth day were the most important. We made a cake using ground corn. We dug a big hole in the ground, and we baked the cake. I had to bless the cake with corn pollen, and then we offered a piece to the sun. The ladies washed my hair in yucca. They did this to keep me pure. The last night, there was singing and praying. I had to stay up all night. I had to behave like a young lady. The *kinaaldá* gave me strength, and it taught me how to be a woman. Now I am able to endure."

The women interviewed for this book conveyed deep emotion when describing their *kinaaldás*. Some revealed eagerness and enthusiasm. Others, moved by the ceremony, sobbed deeply. Through the ceremony, they felt they had acquired a strength that carried them through difficult times later in life. For many Diné women, participating in a *kinaaldá* is a remarkable milestone. Goodwin shared that it is a common saying, "While white women imagined their wedding day, I daydreamed about my *kinaaldá*."

Through the ceremony, they felt they had acquired a strength that carried them through difficult times later in life.

Unlike Anglo society, where the time of the first menstruation remained private, in the Navajo *kinaaldá* ritual, the family announces the daughter or granddaughter's first menstruation to the entire community. Relatives and friends come together for this public celebration that reinforced the Navajo respect for fertility and reproduction.[10] The *kinaaldá* ceremony allows women to follow the path into motherhood, a highly respected calling for The People. Changing Woman granted the nurturing instinct, which includes warm-heartedness, compassion, and affection. Embodying the gift of reproduction, she represented the ideal model of mothering for her people, making Diné mothers the core and caretaker of the family and the culture.[11]

"As with women in other cultures, Navajo women work to ensure the transferring of culture from one generation to the next."[12] Using the wisdom of the past and present, Diné women look to the future for life to continue. The mother-child union represents the strongest bond within the culture. After giving birth, a Navajo mother buries her infant's umbilical cord somewhere close to a sheep corral or an outdoor loom, especially if the child is female. The cord acts as a bond to the earth and the home. It connects the baby to sheep and land, and both give life.[13] No matter what the generation, the women's souls remain Diné as they connect to Changing Woman and her teachings.

Sheep and Weaving

Before the arrival of the Spanish conquistadors in the 1600s, Navajo men, women, and children worked the soil. They grew corn, beans, and squash and gathered wild seeds and plants. The men hunted game such as deer, rabbit, and prairie dogs.[14] The Diné depended on and respected the resources from their land.

The introduction of Spanish livestock to the region drastically transformed the lives of the Navajo. "Sheep, goats, horses, and cattle were all central to the evolution of the Diné society and economy, but from the beginning, the sheep mattered the most."[15] For Navajos, this animal created security, providing food and wool. The Spanish *churro* sheep produced greaseless wool, excellent for weaving.[16] Over a period of time, the Diné increased the size of their flocks and secured more land for grazing. Their large herds caused Navajos to be known as strong and prominent people throughout the Southwest.

Over the next centuries, the Diné understood having sheep meant no hunger. Navajo Ella Deal shared, "Out of all of our animals, it is sheep that gives us life." The Diné moved from their summer camp to their winter, spring, and fall camps to allow for better grazing. Men, women, and children tended the sheep, while women also honed their weaving skills. The Santa Fe Trail, which opened during the early 1800s, created a means for trading Navajo blankets with the "outside" world. By the 1880s, railroad expansion enabled the Navajo markets to grow. Trading posts, established by the late 1890s, had Anglo owners urging weavers to create floor rugs instead of blankets, regarded as excellent works of art.

The art of weaving included a spiritual component for Diné weavers. The creation of a rug produced a sense of harmony and beauty. Women crafted rug designs, not drawn on paper or in the soil but in their minds and hearts. Ask a traditional Navajo weaver, "Who taught you to weave?" and she might answer with the name of her maternal grandmother and tell of the religious traditions of Spider Woman, the esteemed Diné deity, who gave weaving to her and to all Navajo weavers. From Spider Woman's teachings, Diné women through the ages have created beautifully intricate rugs.[17]

Women crafted rug designs, not drawn on paper or in the soil but in their minds and hearts.

Most of the women in *Voices of Navajo Mothers and Daughters: Portraits of Beauty* acquired the many skills of weaving from a close relative. The weaver began by shearing wool from the sheep, so the animal stayed cool during the warm summer months. Next, she washed and carded the wool, and spun it into yarn. Searching the nearby fields, she gathered plants for dyeing the yarn. All of these steps must be completed before she can sit at the loom to weave. Among the women in this book, Alice Lee, Helen Gonnie, Lena Yazzie, Alma Klitso White, Elsie D. Nez, and Sylvia Smith began at an early age and supported their families with this artistry. Jean Mann and women from the Rose Williams family had been awarded for their rug creations. "It was often the grandmothers who passed on the skill of weaving to their granddaughters who learned by watching, not by formal instruction. At the same time, grandmothers model and impart traditional values such as hard work, patience, humility, and moderation."[18]

(Back, left to right) Granddaughter Bettina Lynn Swatts, Daughter Arlinda Swatts, Grandmother Betty A. Lee, (Front) Great-grandmother Alice W. Lee, Sanders, Arizona

Chapter 2

The Lee Family

"My life wasn't too different from my mom's life. We would get up in the morning, and like my mom we had no running water or electricity, and no truck."

—Betty Anne Lee, June 9, 2011

Great-grandmother Alice W. Lee, who speaks Navajo exclusively, lives with her daughter Betty Anne near Sanders, Arizona, where sage and juniper trees blanket the landscape. Alice Lee doesn't know where she was born and is not certain of her age. She thinks she might be eighty-two. Alice Lee attended preschool, and then her schooling ceased because her family "wanted her to do more of the sheep herding and helping with the weaving." She would card the wool and look for the horses. The family had no electricity or running water, so she had to help haul water. They did not have much money. They had no vehicle, just a wagon. She probably had only two or three items of clothing to wear. "It was like that back then," explains Betty Anne.

Alice W. Lee

She continues, "When it was time for my mom to marry, my grandmother told my mom to wed this older guy. She picked the guy for my mom. My grandmother said that he would take care of her because he had sheep, and horses, and stuff like that. He was OK money-wise. Then my grandparents made an arrangement with the guy, so that is how my parents got together. Only there was one problem. My mom did not like this guy, but she had to go with him anyway. She was sixteen when she got married. She didn't like the guy because he was older. He was twenty-six."

Betty Anne, age fifty-six, adds, "My life wasn't too different from my mom's life. We would get up in the morning, and like my mom, we had no running water or electricity, and no truck. But we did have a river close by. We would go there and get the water early in the morning. Under a big rock was hot water, and we would use the hot water from there. My mom would tell us to go and get the water because we needed to make food. So we would take our buckets out there, and we would bring the water back to the hogan. We would cook and then go and herd sheep all day long. We would come back all tired and go to sleep. Then we would do the same thing the next day.

"We were lucky to have a river close by. Everybody would be there doing their washing, and somebody would be sitting in the water. Back then, there used to be a whole bunch of water all over the place, and now it is dry. It is all gone. Some places you could dig a hole, and water would come up. We would also get water from the rain to make food. Now the water has bacteria in it. Nobody would say that about our water back then. We could even drink the rainwater.

"We used to do everything by hand. We used to do our laundry at the river and use the washboard just like in the movies. There was a whole bunch of water out there. We would hang up our wet clothes on trees and bushes, let them dry, fold them, and take them back to the house. We had to walk about two miles back to the hogan.

"While we were herding sheep, we used to play and play out there. We would sit on the sheep, and they would haul us around. It was a nice way to get away from the house because my dad was a mean guy to be around. So we would go out there and play on the logs and play with the sheep. I had six siblings; two brothers and four sisters.

"It was hard for me to be raised up. I didn't want my kids to go through what I went through. I wanted them to have a better life than I did. Sometimes we would run out of food. We would not have anything to eat. When we were starting to get hungry, my mom had to hurry and weave a rug. She had to take it to the store and sell it so she could get groceries. The trip to the store was not an easy one-day trip. It was like a week in the wagon to get to the store to sell the rug. It would be about a forty-mile trip to Gallup [New Mexico] in the wagon. She would leave us with tortillas for that week, along with water. We had to take tiny bits each day, and it was to last until she got back. That is how we were, and it was hard. I used to be really, really skinny, and now look at me. I wish I were still that skinny. We had no shoes, and we used to run around without them. We had calluses on our feet, so we would not get cactus stuck in them. There were nine of us in the hogan, and it was crowded.

> "My mom raised us hard."
>
> –Arlinda Swatts

"Lots of times we would only have breakfast and then not eat all day. We got used to not eating all day. If we got hungry, we would chew plants and pick berries and get full on them. When it would rain, we would drink the water from the mud puddles. It used to taste really good. We were like wild animals. We had to live off of nature.

"I was glad to go to boarding school. There, we had enough to eat. I went to school when I was six years old at Mariano Lake, New Mexico. I stayed there until I was in the fourth grade, and then I changed schools. I went to Fort Wingate, also in New Mexico. It was OK. It was good to go to school, and we learned a lot. They used to teach us how to iron clothes, how to fix the house, clean and mop the floor, and everything. In the morning before we went to school, the instructor would come by and check to see if everything was clean, and if it wasn't, then we would have to go back and do it again. Maybe that is why I am so clean now. I learned a lot at boarding school.

"But then my dad moved us all to Idaho, so he could get a job. And then my mom and dad got separated. So my mom was alone with us kids. I went to school a little bit in Idaho, but then we stopped, and I never went again. I only completed the sixth grade.

"When my own daughter, Arlinda, went to school, I really wanted her to go. I have a sister who went to school and college, and I wanted that for Arlinda. I jumped around too much in my schools. I wanted her to go to school so bad. I wanted her to finish high school and then go on to college. That is what I wanted for her. I wanted for her what I did not have for myself. I was strict with my kids because of the way I was raised. I didn't want Arlinda to be like me.

"My mom had so many children that she did not want to deal with all of us. She had her first child when she was seventeen. I wanted to get away from my home. There was too much alcohol and violence. I only had two children, Arlinda and my son. I wanted them close to me. I did not want anybody to touch them. I always had them with me except when they were in school. I really wanted them to have a good life, not the way I had."

Daughter Arlinda affirms, "When my mom would tell me these stories about her childhood, I realized that I had it made. I didn't think that these kinds of things could happen like they did to my mom. We lived in a city in Idaho. Then we moved back to Sanders, Arizona, because my mom was worried about her mom who had returned to the reservation a long time ago."

Arlinda continues, "My mom raised us hard. I was the only daughter, and she was overprotective of me. In Idaho, she would not let me go anywhere with my friends. I could not have phone calls. We had to clean the apartment. In the morning we had chores. We would get up, eat, wash the dishes, sweep the floor, and then vacuum. After that, we would go to school, and come home, and go straight to homework. We could not watch TV. My mom was really strict about that. We lived in an apartment. We did not go out with friends because Mom was really firm about that too."

Betty Anne adds, "Even though we lived in Idaho, I taught Arlinda the traditional Navajo way. We believed in the medicine man and his healing ways. Like if Arlinda went to the zoo, I told her about animals she could look at and those she couldn't. I told her about things she had to stay away from. Now she is teaching those things to her own daughter, Bettina."

Arlinda explains, "I am trying to keep Bettina in the traditional way. She is sixteen years old. She is learning to respect our traditions. When she had her *kinaaldá*, she had to smile and be polite. She was not supposed to chew gum or eat sweet stuff. Her hair was tied in a bundle. It was during the winter, so the ground was hard. It was in the snow, and so she ran in the snow, and she wore the traditional outfit. We were so proud of her.

"I am pleased with her in school too. She is an honor student. I encourage her every day. I went to high school and got a diploma, but I did not go to college. I just started working after high school. Bettina is succeeding in school and doing things that I didn't do. I encourage her to do a good job in school, and to get a career, and to be somebody. I always tell her to go out there and make something of herself. And you know, she does. She wants to be an FBI agent. She wants to take a year off of school, but I tell her that after high school, she should go straight to college. I tell her that if she has a year's gap, she might not go back to school. I am on her all the time to do a good job in school. I watch her. My mom encouraged me, but she did not encourage me enough. She did not tell me to go to college. I don't want that for Bettina. I feel education is very important. I have high expectations for her. I know she will do fine because of what she has done so far."

When Bettina grows up, she says she plans on teaching her own children the importance of education and the Navajo traditions. Bettina adds, "My mom encourages me to succeed and to do things on my own and to be a good person. I am lucky because my great-grandma is here to back my grandma. My grandma is here to back my mom, and my mom is here to back me. Also, I know that all three women back each other up and are here to back me up, too. I learn from all of them. I have three moms, and these moms help me in my life."

2021

"Unfortunately 2020 took a toll on me," Arlinda said. "In the month of December [2020], I lost my uncle, my beloved grandma [Alice Lee], and my beautiful mother [Betty Anne Lee]. It is hard for me to talk about them. I'm still grieving for them, especially the loss of my mom. We were so close. My loving grandmother died of old age. She was ninety-seven." Arlinda's uncle and mother both died of COVID-19. "I have a lot on my plate taking care of my birth father, my stepdad, my brother, and my own little family. Sometimes it is too much. I wish I had more siblings to share some of the responsibility."

Arlinda Swatts

Arlinda's daughter, Bettina, proudly graduated from Northern Arizona University with a degree in biomedical science. She holds two jobs in Flagstaff, one in a clothing store and the other at a nursing home. Arlinda's other three children are doing well. Her son also graduated from college with the same degree as Bettina. Her third child is in college now in Flagstaff, and her youngest daughter, a seventh grader, is at home. Arlinda visits her children in Flagstaff every other weekend because they keep her going. "I still have my days, but am trying to continue with life."

(Left to right) Grandmother Nona Scott, Mother Daisy Scott-Dover, Daughter Deanna Dover, Leupp, Arizona

Chapter 3

The Scott Family

"We were being stewards of the land by caring for the livestock, the cattle, calves, sheep, and lambs."

—Daisy Scott-Dover, May 1, 2010

Daisy Scott-Dover grew up with her seven brothers and one sister in a hogan in the Canyon Diablo area near Leupp, Arizona. Now, only Daisy's mother, Nona Scott, lives at the camp. At age fifty-two, Daisy, who works as an aide in a public school on the reservation, comes to help her mother on some weekdays and every weekend. Nona, now seventy-seven, speaks Navajo exclusively.

Daisy states, "My mom, Nona, was busy with the nine of us. I was the second oldest and the oldest girl. I had a lot of responsibility taking care of the younger kids, but when I was in school, I had to just take care of myself."

Daisy first attended Leupp Boarding School at the age of six. Her mother worried about her leaving home. Daisy says, "My mom told the government lady not to take me because

Daisy Scott-Dover and Nona Scott

I was too young and too small to go to school. The lady said that I was of age, and that I was ready to go. So my parents took me in their wagon.

"I didn't speak English, but my teacher would speak it. We would answer her in Navajo. Nobody knew what was being said to each other, but by about the end of first grade, I started to understand.

"My parents did not have a vehicle, so they could not visit us at school or bring us home. The mode of transportation back then during the 1960s were wagons and horses. You did not see vehicles. My parents would bring us to school in the fall and pick us up at the start of summer. At Thanksgiving and Christmas the school would bring us home in their vehicles. I went to the boarding school from beginners or kindergarten to the eighth grade. Then I moved to Flagstaff, lived in the Indian dorm, and attended school there."

Once Nona realized that Daisy would be OK at school, she felt relief. Daisy translates for her mom: "I had heard it was good for kids because they would be able to make their way in the world. They would learn to speak English and learn the white man's ways. So I was glad for my kids, and I wanted them to be able to do that. I figured this is how they were going to make their life, and it would help them later on. Their lives were different than mine. I was working at home caring for my kids and the livestock. Daisy was in school learning to speak English and getting an education."

Daisy described summer as a fun time. At home during vacation, Daisy and her sister would play school. Daisy wanted to be the teacher. "I would bring paper from school, and we would cut, color, and draw on the paper. Then we would make envelopes, and we would pretend we were going to the post office. Actually we would walk toward the railroad tracks that were close by our hogan. The rabbitbrush and the four-wing saltbushes were our post office, and we would pin our notes on the bushes."

Daisy's mom remembered when the children would break soda-pop bottles. Daisy states, "We would break off the necks and those would be our horses. We would build small

Nona Scott

corrals and play with bottleneck horses in there. Other times we would cut evaporated milk cans and put them on the front of our shoes and on our heels. We pretended they were like high heels!"

Daisy continues, "My mom taught us a lot about the Navajo ways. In grinding corn I did not use the stones—the *metate* and *mano*—I used a corn grinder to make blue corn meal, blue corn mush, and blue corn pancakes. We would do the [sheep] shearing every year in the spring. We used the big shears that are like those big scissors. We were being stewards of the land by caring for the livestock—the cattle, calves, sheep, and lambs. We tagged the sheep and earmarked them. We went to the sheep camp and cut their tails and gave them their shots. My brother and I always did the roundup."

> "I was working at home caring for my kids and the livestock. Daisy was in school learning to speak English and getting an education."
>
> –Nona Scott

Nona feels great pride in what Daisy has become. With tears in Daisy's eyes, she shares her mother's words. "I pretty much let what Daisy wanted to be up to her. There are a lot of careers for her to do, and I did not tell her to be this or that. I wanted her to be independent and let her decide. She is a wonderful person who knows a lot of things. Whatever she puts her mind to, she accomplishes."

For her own daughter, DeAnna, Daisy stresses education. "I homeschooled my kids because they were ready to learn. Even though DeAnna was four, I knew she was ready for school. I went before the school board to get her in, and at first they said no. I pushed and pushed and said that I would have her tested to prove that she was ready for school.

Finally they decided to accept her, and she was in the top of her class. I told her always to go to school, do her best, and be on the honor roll. I had high expectations for my three children."

Daisy adds, "With me, it was really hard. I was bilingual. Navajo was my first language, so the vocabulary was really hard for me. I would ask myself, 'What does the teacher want?' I was really shy, and I didn't raise my hand. I did not want my kids to go through what I went through, so I only spoke English to them. I did this because I did not want them to struggle like I did. Now I speak Navajo to them. They are picking it up a little.

"Whatever my kids wanted, I always got it for them. I did not want them to have a hard childhood like I did. We had to make our own toys. We had to come up with what we had at hand. I didn't want to deprive my kids. My daughter would play with Barbie dolls, and we had a lot of books. We had more books than toys.

"DeAnna had a good childhood. There was a great difference between her childhood and mine. I had to work harder. I had to take care of my brothers and sister while my parents went to the migrant fields to pick the vegetables. We would be here with our grandparents, and we had to make sure that we had enough food and clean clothes. We had to look out for everyone's welfare. We had to take care of the sheep and livestock. When there was no water, we had to take our sheep to the water in the canyon. We had to pump water for the sheep. It was an all-day thing. I had more responsibility. We did not have the convenience of running water and electricity. DeAnna had TV and lights and hot water. Everything was more modernized for her. We traveled to Los Angeles and to the amusement parks and museums. She was being exposed to more things. Just the exposure made a difference. I was on the reservation, and the only time we would go anywhere would be when we took a school field trip. Maybe we would go to Flagstaff or Phoenix.

"My dad left my mom when I was in the fourth grade. So we had it hard. We were on welfare, and with nine kids it was really rough. After my dad left, my mom had to go to a lot of places to pick vegetables. She went to Idaho for potatoes and to southern Arizona to pick cucumbers and cantaloupe. My grandparents took care of us. Our childhood was being on welfare, and we all said that we would get jobs and never be on welfare. We had no vehicle until we each went on our own.

"When it came time for DeAnna's *kinaaldá*, she did not want one. Her grandmother had one," explains Daisy, "where she did the running and grinding the corn to make the cake. I did not have one because I was away at school, but I really wanted DeAnna to have one.

> "Whatever my kids wanted, I always got it for them. I did not want them to have a hard childhood like I did. We had to make our own toys. . . . I didn't want to deprive my kids."
>
> –Daisy Scott-Dover

"I wanted a *kinaaldá* for her, but she was dead set against it. She was afraid it would be like a Navajo ceremony, like a Blessingway or Enemy Way. Those are both healing ceremonies. We go to church, and we are Christian. I told her that it is only a ceremony if the medicine man is there with his prayers, and he won't be there. I wanted it from the Bible perspective on how to be a virtuous lady, on how to be a young woman and an acceptable young lady. I wanted her to know that you conduct yourself in a suitable manner and behavior. One of these days she will have her own home and clean, cook, and sew. She will have to know how to care for her family. She should find a lady who she looks up to, who she admires who has had motherhood. I wanted that for her. We can leave out the prayers and the medicine man. But at least have ladies from the church come over and share their wisdom for her on how to be a lady, and to do the running and the grinding and the making of the cake. That is our tradition as Navajos. But at this time the whole idea of her becoming a young woman was frightening to her. All the while I am talking to DeAnna, she is crying, 'No! No! No! No! I don't want it done! I don't want it done!' When she was asked today at age twenty-three if she is still fine with saying no, her response is that she is still glad she did not have a *kinaaldá*."

What Daisy also wanted for DeAnna "was for her to be in a profession where she can earn a lot of money and where she has a job that she truly enjoys—perhaps a career in computers or another high-paying job. Today she is doing just that. She works for a company in Flagstaff, and she is a fashion model."

DeAnna adds, "When I was younger, I always spent time at my grandmother's camp. Now that I am older, I do not come out much. I spend my time in Flagstaff and travel around the country. But now that I am in my twenties, I am learning to appreciate my grandmother and her customs more, even though I feel somewhat removed from all of it."

2021

DeAnna shared that Grandmother Nona never liked to be photographed. She would shy away from cameras. The only reason she allowed herself to be photographed for this project was because Daisy and DeAnna requested it. Reluctantly Nona agreed. When she saw the photos, she was so pleased that she framed one and hung it in her home.

Sadly, Nona Scott passed away in 2016. Daisy, after several attempts to retire from education, did so during the spring of 2021. She returned several times because the school needed her expertise. DeAnna declared, "This time my mom's retirement is for real!" Daisy acts as fire support and cook for Fire Shots, a firefighting team. Daisy and DeAnna live at Nona's camp, and DeAnna commutes to Flagstaff for work at a medical company. She gave up modeling a few years ago.

Nona Scott, Deanna Dover

Mother Bertha Fuson and Daughter Jennie Haag, Dilkon, Arizona

Chapter 4

The Fuson Family

"I was to plant in a straight line to a fence. I did my best. So in the summer the corn started to come up, and my row was all wavy and crooked! My mom always laughed about that."

—Jennie Fuson Haag, July, 17, 2009

On a wide span of fields with red buttes in the background near Dilkon, Arizona,* stands Bertha Fuson's family's camp. Her fifty-nine-year-old daughter, Jennie, declares, "This countryside was first given to my mom's family in the late 1800s. Her great-grandmother and many others were captured and forced by Kit Carson and his army to walk to Fort Sumner, New Mexico. It was a difficult journey, known as The Long Walk. [see Chapter 23] Carson had cleared the area where our people lived because the federal government said our people were raiding too much. Some soldiers thought there also might be gold on our land, and they wanted to see if it was really there. Those Navajos who survived the march and the stay [at Fort Sumner] were allowed to return four years later to what is now our reservation."

Bertha Fuson

Jennie continues, "My mom's great-grandmother, who was a Hopi Indian, returned to the Jeddito, Arizona, area where she raised her children. One of her descendants, my grandmother, got married, and her husband brought her to Dilkon, Arizona. Later the federal government designated this Dilkon countryside to be hers. Navajos are a matriarchal society, so my mom was given our land.

"Eighty-six years ago, my grandmother gave birth to my mom on this land in our hogan near a butte. My mom, who does not speak English, has spent her entire life in this region." This vast acreage gives miles of grass for her family's livestock. Her family would move several times a year to give the sheep and cattle nourishment. "We moved mostly in the summer, but in the winter we would settle down and just stay in one place," explains Jennie.

Bertha's family had many sheep, and Bertha grew up herding them with her older sister, Betty. "One day, while herding sheep near an area called Elephant Butte, they heard a strange noise and wondered what it was. They looked toward the sound and saw something moving in the distance. They could not make out what it was, and they were getting scared, so they hid behind a hill. They found out later that it was a car. They had just seen their first vehicle!

"Not only did my mom herd sheep, but as a child she also learned how to shear, card wool and spin it into yarn, make looms, and weave rugs. She did this for many years. Then, in the spring of 1938, she was arranged in marriage to Joe Fuson, who lived in Tolani Lake, Arizona. At this time she was fifteen, and her husband-to-be was sixteen," says Jennie. "My dad came on horseback and his family traveled in a wagon. After the wedding it was raining, and the roads were muddy when they started out to where they were going to live. They brought with them six horses, one cow, a concho belt, and ten dollars, which at the time was like a hundred dollars to them."

Bertha and her husband had six daughters and three sons, with Jennie being fourth from the oldest. She adds, "I was born in a *cha'a'oh* [shade house]. I was told that during my

Bertha Fuson

birth, three or four women sat around in the shelter waiting and when it was time, they helped with my birth." Now Jennie lives in Flagstaff and comes to Dilkon to help her elderly mother and father every other week. Jennie assists by gathering firewood, hauling water, and cooking. When lambing season occurs, she is there at their camp. She also acts as their interpreter when necessary.

Jennie translates for her mom, "When my daughter was growing up, she was a good little girl. She wasn't naughty. She spent a lot of time playing by herself. She would pick up sticks and rocks and have fun with them. These sticks and rocks were like her toys. She would play make-believe. Jennie would say this rock is this, and this stick is that. Back then, we did not have store toys. There was a lot of pretending going on with the rocks and sticks."

Jennie adds, "I remember a funny story when I was six years old. My mom and dad started a cornfield, and they were planting. I did not know anything about cornfields. I was watching them. My mom had my baby sister with her, and the baby started crying. My mom had to go to her, so she explained to me quickly how to plant corn. She told me to dig a small hole and put in a few corn. I was to plant in a straight line to a fence. I did my best. So in the summer the corn started to come up, and my row was all wavy and crooked! My mom always laughed about that."

Bertha continues, "Kids back then were not like kids today. Kids back then did what they were told. They listened to their mother and their father and their grandparents. Kids grew up with everybody there living close by, like your aunts and their kids. Everybody was around. If your aunt asked you to do something, then you would do it. It was the same with your grandparents. Kids today have to be entertained. They need too much attention. My kids didn't need too much attention."

At the age of six, Jennie attended a boarding school in Steamboat, Arizona. She says, "A Navajo man from the Bureau of Indian Affairs from the federal government came to my camp and took me and my cousin to school. My aunt was at my home along with my cousin. My mom wasn't home at the time. When she came home she found out I was taken to school. But that was OK with her because an education was what she wanted for me.

"First the school man was coming for another cousin who lived close by. Her parents enrolled her, and they told him that there were two girls nearby who needed to go to school too. That was my cousin and me. They said we were the right age to go to school. Then the man came to our camp to take us to school. Since my aunt was with me at the time, she filled out the papers. Then she grabbed some of my clothes and put them in a bag. It was late in the day, and we were the last to be picked up. They put us in a station wagon and took us to the school in Steamboat, Arizona. We weren't crying. We just kind of went. When we got there, it was dark, and the other kids were asleep.

"In the morning we had breakfast and went to class. School had already started and was in session for a few weeks. I don't remember that first class at all. I must have been in kindergarten. I just knew that the teacher talked English, and every student spoke Navajo.

"After class we went back to the dormitory. When we got there, a lady asked us a question in Navajo. She wanted to know if we wore a 'long skirt' or a 'short skirt'? I didn't know what she was talking about. I didn't understand what she was asking, so I just said, 'short skirt.' I found out later that the 'short skirt' meant that we were Presbyterian. The 'long skirt' meant that we would be Catholic because the nuns wore the long robes. I said 'short skirt' because my mom wore her skirts mid-calf, so I chose what my mom had. I was sent to the Presbyterian Church while I was at that school.

"During first grade I do remember the teacher and being in the classroom. The teacher was reading that Dick and Jane book. She would read from there, and then she would put questions on the board. I remember sitting there thinking, 'What is this?' I had no idea what she wanted. Throughout the year, I would start to pick up words. I then began to answer the teacher's questions. I am sure they were one-word answers. In second grade I started to pick up some more English, and then by third grade I was almost fluent. There was a girl in my class, and she spoke a lot of English, so she and I would talk back and forth, and that helped me a lot.

"At Steamboat, we would only come home at Christmas and summer. Always at the end of summer I would ask my mom if I could stay at home. The school was so far away; I hated to go. I used to say that I did not want to go back, and my mom would say, 'No, you go back to school.' My mom wanted me to have an education because she didn't have one. She told me that if I had an education, then later I could support myself. I did what my mom wanted me to do. My mom always made sure everybody got an education. By fourth grade I changed schools. I was closer to my house, and I spoke English. By then, I was finally OK with being away from home.

> "My mom is a gentle, patient, and strong person. She knew what she wanted for us and that was having her children be educated."
>
> –Jennie Haag

"My oldest sister didn't go to school until she was thirteen or fourteen. A man came ahead of time and had my mom sign papers to enroll her. This way her going to school would not be a surprise. She would know ahead of time. It was at the Intermountain School in Utah. They had my sister go to a five-year program where they would teach a little bit of English. She spoke only Navajo until she was thirteen. Also, they would teach her some kind of

Bertha Fuson

vocation, so that she could have a job. Her vocation was housekeeping. She ended up working for Ganado Hospital in Ganado, Arizona.

"My mom didn't go to school. She was told that she needed to help around the house, do the chores, and watch the sheep. She and her older half-sister would tend to the sheep. When she wanted to enroll in school, her parents told her no. Where my mom was willing for us to get an education, her parents were not willing for her to get one. She wanted something different for us. My mom is a gentle, patient, and strong person. She knew what she wanted for us and that was having her children be educated."

Jennie's feelings of a close connection with her mother comes through in the words she shared during Bertha Fuson's funeral in 2011. She describes her mother as a "great lady, strong, wise, loving, and generous. She never turns people away when they come for mutton, if she has it to give. She is gentle. She is patient. When teased by someone, she always has a comeback, never a loss for words. My mother stands tall, smiles with pride, always greets people she knows, and never lets them get away without being acknowledged. Her only regret is that she never got an education."

2021

Jennie shared, "I lived in the Native American dorm in Flagstaff while attending Flagstaff High School and graduated in 1967. I now reside in Flagstaff with my dentist husband. We have two sons, both married. Our older son has a daughter, and they live in Massachusetts. Our other son lives in Bayfield, Colorado. My mother, Bertha Fuson, died in December of 2011 at the age of eighty-eight. My sisters and I took care of our father at the Dilkon homestead until he went into a Winslow nursing home where we visit him. He is ninety-eight years old."

*Dilcon Boarding School is located in Dilkon, Arizona. When Dilcon Boarding School was established in 1962, the government mistakenly spelled it Dilcon instead of Dilkon.

Mother Lena Yazzie and Daughter Kim Yazzie, Sanders, Arizona

Chapter 5

The Yazzie Family

"What you are doing is pushing yourself. You are making yourself strong. You are building up your lungs and mind. You don't know what is happening down the road. You are preparing yourself for those things."

—Kim Yazzie, June 7, 2011

Lena Yazzie describes her childhood as difficult. The last thing she wants is for her four children to grow up like she did. "I was a child left behind. I don't want my girls to follow in my footsteps because I had it rough. My dad was not there. He left us when I was two. I never had a chance to have a father figure. My mom did not speak English, and we did not have any transportation. Education was all I had.

"For school I first went to the Navajo Gospel Mission near Pinon, Arizona. All I knew was how to pray and sing and herd sheep. And I knew about the Bible. I did not know that there were other things going on elsewhere. But then my mom could not afford the school, and I did not have a sponsor. So I had to go to Tuba City Boarding School. I did not like it my first year there. I thought God was punishing me. The boarding school was a place I called 'hell.' I was so sad. But I somehow managed to make it through. They made everyone leave the school and go home for Christmas break, and then we had to leave for summer break too. So from September to December, I was without contact with my mom and from January to May with no contact too. It was really hard on me, especially when I was young. As I got older, I was more independent. I used to catch rides with neighbors, and they would take me to school. And when I got there, I would check myself into the dorm.

"My children have both of their parents. That is one way my kids have it different. I never worked outside of the home after I got married. I married at age nineteen. That was pretty young. I had my first daughter when I was twenty. I just barely got out of school and started a family. My husband was more like a father to me. He was four years older. My three girls are very close to their dad. That is another way my childhood is different from theirs.

"In the old way, the man is supposed to be out there hunting for food, and the wife is supposed to prepare the food, and keep the home warm, and the house clean. My husband told me the day I got married that I was not going to work. I was going to stay home and raise our kids. He believed that a woman should stay home and do the rug weaving. But I did not know how to do rug weaving. I would see my mom weave, but she never would say, 'Come over here, and sit, and learn to weave.' But I would watch her, and so I learned.

"My husband was bringing home the income, so I stayed with my kids, and I would go to their day-school when stuff was going on. I would always be there for my kids, all four of them. Once on the school bus, they got in a fight with one of the kids. After that, they never took the bus again. So every day I had to take my kids to school in the morning and bring them home in the evening.

"My mom never checked on me. With my kids I am going a different route. Just because I lived that childhood, doesn't mean I am going to punish my own kids. So I give them a lot of attention. I checked on my daughter Kim every other day at school. I would sit in class and see how she was doing. I wanted to make her safe and to see that she was OK or if she was having problems. I wanted all of my kids to be protected."

Even though Kim had a great deal of support, she still had a difficult time adjusting to school. Lena describes the situation. "Kim had a rough time in first and second grade because of the language. She knew how to speak Navajo, and the sad part was that she knew no English. I put her in school, and she had the hardest time. In preschool everybody spoke Navajo. She could sing in Navajo and talk to the grandmas and grandpas. But when she got to first grade, man-oh-man did she have a hard time! She would cry and say, 'Mama, I don't know how to talk English.' All of the kids would make fun of her. It was really bad, until she got into the third grade. From then on she did fine."

> "My husband told me the day I got married that I was not going to work. I was going to stay home and raise our kids."
>
> –Lena Yazzie

Kim adds, "From kindergarten to second grade I spoke only Navajo. They put me in a bilingual classroom, and then they would switch me to a straight English classroom. Then they would put me back into a bilingual classroom. I was more comfortable in the bilingual classroom, but then they put me back into an English classroom, and I started to learn English. Then they put me back in bilingual again. Back and forth I went. By then I started to let go of the Navajo and learn English. Finally my mom said to keep me in the 'English only' side, and gradually I lost my Navajo. I could not speak it anymore. In my mind I wanted to say things in Navajo, but when it tried to come out, it just wasn't there. Now as an adult and a teacher at Valley High School in Sanders, it is coming back to me. The high school helped me. Here at home my mom and dad talk to me in Navajo, but

Lena Yazzie and Kim Yazzie

I can't go on and on in Navajo. When I speak, it is choppy. When we go to dinners and everybody is talking in Navajo, everyone starts laughing at me. The joke is on me when I speak Navajo."

Another way that Kim and Lena's lives have been different is that Kim had a *kinaaldá*. Lena, being Christian, did not know what a *kinaaldá* was, but later she learned. Lena states, "You are supposed to have the ceremony right when the menstruation cycle begins. Right then and there. Kim got it one morning, so I told her it is time. I called my father-in-law and said we are not going to wait. Nowadays, people wait. Some families say let's wait for spring break or when school is out. Not us!

"In a *kinaaldá* the young woman is to stand up straight, and she is not to laugh for any reason. She is to be a lady and be serious. She is to be nice when people talk to her. She is to listen and do what she is told. She has to run many miles and dress traditionally for four days. My father-in-law came over and told us that we were going to do everything right. School was going on, but he said that she could catch up with school. So we took her out for four days. He is not the type to say, 'OK, let's wait.' We got everything done right away."

Kim shares, "From the ladies you learn how to be a woman. Your back was to be straight, chest out, and stomach in. You would have thought that my mom would have been with me in the hogan, but it was the opposite. They told her to stay in the house and cook. My dad was at my side. He told me the stories and explained why I was having this ceremony.

"Every morning you have to wear a sash belt* around your waist, to mold your tummy and hold it in, and you have to tie it tight on you. Also, you are running three times a day—once in the morning, once in the afternoon, and once in the evening. The first day you run only a mile. Tomorrow you run another mile farther. The next day, add another mile, and so on, and by the last day you run about four miles. What you are doing is pushing yourself. You are making yourself strong. You are building up your lungs and pushing your mind. You don't know what is going to happen down the road. You are preparing yourself for those things.

"Standing tall with good posture is another thing you are supposed to look at. People who came from The Long Walk stood up and were strong enough. Imagine how many miles they must have walked. They had babies and things to carry. That is what you are representing. You are taking the process of Changing Woman and what she went through. For those four days, I could not eat sweets. I could not eat candy, or pop, or salt, just bread and water. That is it. When the menstrual cycle comes and if you eat salt, then you get bloated. Doctors never tell you this. It is easier when you don't have these things.

> "My dad always said that when you do something good, you always come back and say thank you."
>
> –Kim Yazzie

"Many times I remember my dad was saying to me to fix my hair. 'Don't let it dangle. The only time you can let your hair stringy is when you are having a *kinaaldá*.'" Kim continues, "When you are having your *kinaaldá*, they tie the front part up, and the rest hangs down. Also, when we were growing up, my dad would have us run in the morning, so he was already preparing us for that *kinaaldá* day. He would come to our door at five in the morning with a wet washcloth and put it on us. We would jump up, and he would say, 'Let's go running, girls!' When we would come back, he would say, 'Go bless yourself. Let the sun touch you four times.'

"The wisdom, the strength, and the knowledge come from being part of those four days. I believe it has taken me a long ways, especially when I went off to college. I would be alone there. Talk about culture shock! It was hard, and it was stressful, but I got through it. Looking back on my *kinaaldá*, I had it for a reason. It was to prepare me.

"I had this school assignment. I wondered how I was going to complete it because I only had one week. I would be crying. How can I get this done? I would call home crying to my mom. She would say, 'You're going to finish this.' She would talk to me for the longest time.

"My dad would talk to me too, and he would say, 'Go run, go run!' Running would take me back to my traditional time, and singing too, and repeating my name. When you are in a *kinaaldá*, you are constantly introducing yourself over and over. You are constantly telling people who you are, who your clan is, and where you come from.

"When I would call at college and I was upset, my dad would say, 'Say your name four times,' and that would get me back to the basics again. I would tell him 'OK', and do it. Then I would start to work, and it would go fine. My dad always said that when you do something good, you always come back and say thank you. Say thank you back to Mother Nature. It doesn't have to be big. It can be a pinch of corn pollen to say thank you."

Because Kim's mother emphasized education, Kim attended college and now teaches agriculture at Valley High School. Lena stressed to all of her children, "You are to go farther than I did in school. You should get a job and learn to support yourself. Don't settle down early. Don't get involved with anybody. You should have time to go out and see the world. And they did that. Then when you are older you can settle down. Today my children live close to me. I really like that. I did not want to do to my children what my mother and father did to me. I am proud of my children." To Kim, her mother is a beautiful, strong person who never gives up.

2021

Kim works with a food service company based in San Antonio, Texas. "I'm a marketing specialist for a program by Labott Foods called the Native American Beef Program," she stated. "I left teaching after being awarded the 2012 Outstanding Young Member of the Arizona Agriculture Teachers Association. Today I work with 850 families from 52 Native American ranches. This has been an amazing project to be part of, a program that creates economic development for tribal communities and to carry the culture, the traditional Diné way of life.

Kim Yazzie

"In the past six years I've been busy building and protecting a brand that has created a major impact all across Indian country. It's nice to see our grassroots people raise quality stock, become progressive producers, connect them to field yards, food distributors, and onto some amazing chefs. At the same time they are able to take their families to enjoy a nice steak, raised from generation to generation.

"My daughter, Tyann Kaycu Layton, is now twelve years old. She is my world. She tends to amaze me every day. Her interest, along with my career, seem opposite, but very familiar too. She's been a School Princess at Pine Springs Day School and is now the current Miss Wide Ruins Community School Princess. Sometimes I think she values our culture and traditions and Diné way of life more than I do.

"She reminds me, 'We're only here for a little while. Believe, smile, enjoy life, Mom.'

"I often tell her, 'You are wise beyond your years!' She's an A honor student, athletic, in 4-H—lambs, poultry, rabbits, horses—and rodeo with barrel racing. She's done some amazing accomplishments, and she loves to bake and teach."

When asked if she was still weaving, Kim's mother, Lena, answered, "I have not been weaving lately, the way I used to weave. My hands sometimes get arthritis, and my knees are bad when sitting on the floor. Now today I have a three-by-four [rug], and I am barely starting it. It's been up for a while. Hopefully I will get it done this year."

*A sash belt is a woven belt used to control a woman's figure and as a support during childbirth. The belt is offered as a gift when a young woman has her first *kinaaldá*.

Mother Rebecca N. Zee and Daughter Maye Zee, Tuba City, Arizona

Chapter 6

The Zee Family

"After [my mom] had her children, she brought their placentas home too. She placed each one in a special tree. When my children were born, she did the same thing. And when my grandkids were born, I did the same thing too."

—Maye Zee, October 15, 2011

Rebecca N. Zee, a traditional woman who speaks Navajo exclusively, always laughs when she gives her age. She says she might be seventy-six, but she isn't sure. Her daughter, Maye Zee, explains, "We were not certain when she was really born, so we just made up a birthdate of January 1, 1934." Maye continues, "I am fifty-two years old and was born in 1959. Both my mom and I were born in a hogan. My mom was born on Hopi land, but her family did not know it was Hopi land. I was born on the Hopi partitioned land near Big Mountain, Arizona. This is the land that was given to the Hopis because of the Navajo-Hopi Land Dispute." (see Chapter 23)

Rebecca N. Zee

Maye continues Rebecca's story. "My mom tells me that when she was young, she spent most of her time herding sheep, but she also had an area which was her playground. Her toys were sticks used to make horses, and rocks shaped like babies made into pretend dolls. Sometimes my mom would just tie a scarf around a rock and carry it around like it was her baby. Other times my mom and her cousin would pretend to make a cake, like they were having a *kinaaldá*. They would use soil to make the cake. Looking for yellow-colored rocks, they would use them as corn. They would pretend to grind the corn to make pudding for the *kinaaldá*. They would build a fire on the make-believe cake. While they were playing, my mom's brothers would sneak up and tease them.

"My mom had the old way of marriage. It was an arranged marriage. My mom and dad were married when they were eighteen or nineteen. They were both the same age. You see, there were two brothers. One brother married my mom, and the other brother married her sister, Maryanne. The older brother married Maryanne first. And then he told his brother, who turned out later to be my dad, that there was a special lady who was Maryanne's sister. My dad decided to go and meet this special lady. But instead of meeting her, he only got to see her. When he saw her, he liked her. So later my dad's parents came over to see if my mom and dad could get together. But nobody told my mom until a day or two before the wedding. My grandparents told my mom that she did not have a choice. She could not say no because it had already been arranged and planned. My dad told me that back then women were not too expensive, that his family only had to pay three horses for my mom.

"Once the horses were given to my grandfather, my uncle and my grandpa got into a fight over the horses because my uncle really wanted one of them. Horses must have been scarce back then. But my dad did not give him one. And so the trade was made, three horses for one bride. I asked my mom if she was scared to marry. She told me that she wasn't because she did not have a choice. She knew that she just had to get to know this man who was to be her husband."

Maye Zee talks about her childhood and how different it was from how she lives today. "When I was a small girl, we had no car, but we did have a wagon. Later on, we got a truck. I would ride horses when I would herd sheep. Also, my brothers, sisters, and I had many different playground areas. We would build tree houses and pretend we were making food. We would keep cans as toys and use plastic liter bottles for dolls. Even though we had time to play, most of the time we were herding sheep. We were doing these things when we came home from boarding school during the summer. We never lived in a house. We had two hogans, a winter one and a summer one. They were in different parts of our land. In the fall we would move down to the cornfields and harvest the corn. We would sleep in a little hogan or shed, or we would sleep outside or in the bed of our truck or the wagon.

"I went to Rocky Ridge School just for first grade. It was not a big school, and I could live at home. Back in the day they did not have bus stops like now. I had to walk two miles to the bus stop. That was difficult to do, so then for second grade my parents put me in the Tuba City Boarding School, and I had to live in the dorm. I had to face all of the bullies there. Some of the dorm mothers were mean. When my mom and dad would take me to school, I would cry when they left. I even had to have the principal hold onto me when they had to leave because I was crying so hard.

"We never lived in a house. We had two hogans, a winter one and a summer one. They were in different parts of our land."
–Maye Zee

"It was difficult for me to go to boarding school. I never liked it. I wanted to be home. It was quite a ways for my mom and dad to visit. They did not come and see me often. That was sad. I lived in the dorm and missed a lot of school days. I was sick because I wanted my parents and my home. Later, when I was older, my parents kept talking to me about my own needs and how important school was. I knew I did not have a choice. I had to go to school.

"My mom did not feel sad when I went to school. She left me at the dorm. I was crying and crying after her. But she did not feel sad because she wanted me to go to school and get a good education. She wanted me to have good teachers. She told my dad that I had no business being at home. I belonged at school to get educated. And that is exactly what happened. Now I have a good job. I was the only one in my family who got a good education and a good job. Now I help my family all I can.

"School was the same for my mom, only she went when she was older. Back in the day the only school they had for her was Intermountain Boarding School in Utah. She went for only one year because she got really lonely and homesick and did not want to go back. She must have been twelve years old when she went, and she did not like it. It was a mission school. She wanted to stay home with her mom and her dad. She said that she would rather herd sheep. When I was a child, I felt the same way my mom did about school.

"We had our breaks from school at Thanksgiving and Christmas. The summertime was the only period when my brothers and sisters and I went home. At home we weren't allowed to sleep in. We had no TV and no phone. I remember we only had one radio station we could listen to. It was KOMA, Oklahoma City. We would listen to it late at night. Man, that station would pull us through. Way late at night, I had that little radio. We loved to listen to the music.

"We would have breakfast early in the morning. We were required to start preparing food and cooking at an early age of seven or eight. We were taught to make the dough and the bread. We were required to make breakfast, lunch, and dinner. Nobody felt sorry for us if we were sick or lazy. There was no such thing as being lazy. We would go during the early morning hours and herd the sheep and be back by ten in the morning before it got hot.

"And then I always said we were required to be responsible at an early age of eight or nine. My parents would go off to a squaw dance or ceremony. And we kids would stay at home. There was a big responsibility on our shoulders, especially if you were a girl. You had to cook for the boys. Boys had to haul the firewood. We had to make bread for the boys. There was no mercy! Water was scarce. Whatever water we had was from a barrel. We had to conserve. We would not take daily showers. We were lucky if we could take showers once a week. We would maybe take a sponge bath. We just had to conserve.

"Going to the store to get treats just did not happen; however, my paternal grandma was always good about storing treats. She would hide them away in big trunks, or maybe five or six suitcases. And when she needed your help, it would be like earning a treat. If you would go to her hogan, she would ask you to wash dishes. Then she would ask you to straighten up or clean the floor, and she would give you a soda or Cracker Jacks.

"We did not have a cookstove. We had a barrel for a stove. We made fry bread and tortillas. We always had fresh mutton in the winter. People were always nice back in the day. Your neighbor would butcher, and then you would get a piece of meat from them. They would always share. Besides meat we would have winter squash. But I would say our main dish was potatoes. My dad made really good potato soup.

"My mom and dad had seasonal jobs. Sometimes they would leave for a while. They would go away to Cedar City, Utah. They would work in the fields up there. Sometimes we would get bags and bags of potatoes from there when they would come home. We used to have them in storage. It was in the ground and really, really cold because we did not have a refrigerator. It was like a dungeon. They would store all of their corn, squash, and beans in there.

"We would get our flour from the trading post. The closest trading post was Red Lake. From here I would say that it was twenty-five miles. We would also go to Rocky Ridge Trading Post. We would get coffee, meat, lard, shortening, and canned goods.

“I must have been twelve years old when I had my *kinaaldá*. Back in the day, all of the ladies were strict. You had to do it when your period happened then and there. There was no planning, no setting dates. I was lucky to have mine in warm weather. I had to grind corn on the grinding stones. It was really a strict *kinaaldá* compared to nowadays. Back then, even my diet was important—no greasy foods, no salt, no sugar, and no sweets of any kind for four days. At the beginning of my first day, my hair was tied. They would pick a certain person to do it. Mine was my paternal grandmother. She told me how to act and how to be. She was really stern about everything. She was a sweet lady, but she wanted the *kinaaldá* done properly. I had to run every morning and late in the evening for the four days. I had to be pure with all of the salt and sugar out of my body. This allowed me to run better. I would grind the corn for four days. The last night I had to stay up all night. The medicine man came and sang for me. I mixed the corn, and made the pudding, and baked it in the ground overnight, so it became a cake. Everyone shared the cake except for me.”

Maye Zee

Maye continues, “When I was older, my mom was there when I had my children. She was with me for each birth. She asked for the placenta for each and every one of them. After she had her children, she brought their placentas home too. She placed each one in a special tree. When my children were born, she did the same thing. And when my grandkids were born, I did the same thing too. When you leave the hospital, the nurse would just throw the placenta away, or she burned it. My mom and I did not want that. The placenta is part of the baby. And when you bring the placenta home, you will always know where your home is, where you are from, and where you belong. It is kind of like a connection. This is so the children do not forget. This is so they will always know where their home is. For my children and grandkids, I wrapped up each placenta and put it on the tree. You wrap it real good in a cloth and place it in a branch. My kids' placentas and my grandkids' placentas were put in the same tree as mine and my mother's other children.

"Back in the day, my mom was a real healthy woman and strong. She worked like a man. She was always behind my dad. She worked with him. She is real loving and is kind of like me. If she wants to say something to you, she doesn't beat around the bush. She was that kind of woman. But she has mellowed out in her old age. She still stands her ground. If she doesn't like what you are doing, she will correct you. She is softer to her grandchildren than she was with us growing up. And I always tell her that was not fair!"

"She would like my children and my grandchildren to carry on what we know and have learned."

–Maye Zee

Maye translates for Rebecca, "I was kind of strict and mean. I tell Maye that she has come this far. She is a good mother and a grandmother. I appreciate what I see in Maye now. I see what I have taught her."

Maye adds, "But sometimes when I am getting after my kids, she tells me to chill out and be soft with them. She still kind of corrects me, but she likes what she sees in me, being a leader and doing what I have to do for the family. The main thing that my mom wants us to carry on is what she taught us about being a woman. She would like my children and my grandchildren to carry on what we know and have learned. She wants it to keep going and going."

2021

Maye has six grandchildren, three girls and three boys. "They are beautiful and keep me on my toes," she said. In January of 2018, Maye's father died. The grief has been difficult for her mother and her to bear. "But my mother is so amazing and strong, and she's encouraging me to be strong too and that we live out our lives for our children and grandchildren."

COVID-19 tragedy struck many members of Maye's family. "We lost family members. It just spread everywhere. Now we cannot be together. My mom is eighty-five years old, and she caught COVID. My sister came to see my mom, and she was coughing and coughing. Then my mom wasn't feeling well so I took her to Tuba City Hospital. She already had a spot on her lung. I was so upset, but luckily she recovered." Maye herself suffered from COVID but recovered. She continues to work at home for the Navajo Relocation Commission, but longs to retire to spend more time with her mom, children, and grandchildren.

"My mom is now in a nursing home in Phoenix. For a long time she could not see her kids and grandkids. I ache to hug her. I can't do it yet. Now we can visit my mom on the patio in the nursing home, but we cannot touch her. Our whole family cannot be together. We have to quarantine. But we really want to be together."

Mother Marian Yazzie, Daughter Clarissa (Clair) Yazzie, Daughter Ronette Yazzie, Lupton, Arizona

Chapter 7

The Yazzie Family

"My mother was very protective, and I raised my girls with the same protection."

—Marian Yazzie, June 8, 2011

Clair Yazzie, age twenty-five, attended the University of Arizona for a year and had to return home to Lupton, Arizona, because of finances. Her scholarship only paid for one semester. Now she works in the clothing department at JCPenney in Gallup, New Mexico. She wants to return to school one day and pursue medicine. Her sister, Ronette Yazzie, nineteen, travels with the Navajo Nation band. She also taught herself how to make jewelry and pottery, and she is teaching herself how to play the drums. She wants to compose music for the movies. "My dad's side of the family is very musical, and I picked that up too."

The girls' mother, Marian Yazzie, an administrative assistant, has worked for the Sanders School District in Arizona for several years. Also an ordained minister, she studied along with her husband, Ron. The couple met at a Bible college.

Clarissa (Clair) Yazzie and Ronette Yazzie

Marian's own mother had an arranged marriage at age fourteen. "My mother did not have a choice in the person she wanted to marry. Because my mother got married at such a young age, she was very caring of me. My mother was protective, and so I raised my girls with the same protection. My dad was twenty-one. Mom had never seen my dad until the day she got married. But my mom and dad made it through their marriage. Then, my mom passed away when she was fifty-nine years old."

Marian's mother had strong values, and she passed those down to her children. Marian explains, "My mom taught me to respect my elders. I was to always ask if they needed help. Don't just go and do it for them; ask them first. I was trained that responsibility was essential. But my mom did not like animals in the house, and I let them in anyway! Also I was told not to mark on myself or pierce myself."

Education remains central to the Yazzie family. This desire for education began with Marian's mother. Marian says, "My mother, the girl's grandmother, was not favored by her mother." Only one child in the family could go to school because all of the other kids had to stay home and work. Marian's grandmother selected Marian's mother's older sister to attend. Marian's mother had to stay home and tend the sheep. This did not sit well with her; she regretted not being educated. "That is why my own mother pushed us hard to attend and to finish school and to better ourselves."

Marian spent many years in boarding school. "My mom allowed me to be in school when I was six years old. I was taken to the boarding school in a wagon, and the school was about twelve miles away. My mom always talked about wanting an education, even though she did not have an education herself. She would tell us to get used to what needs to happen in school. I was to know where to sit, and I was to obey. It was hard at first, but after a month I got used to it. My story in boarding school was not a negative one. My story was that the school people would feed you in the morning and they would feed you at noon and in the evening. You had a place to stay that was warm, and I was not abused. My parents were not well off.

"In the summer it was hard for us when we were home. It was my mother's encouragement that we made it through all of those boarding school years. My mother strongly supported us. We were not checked out of the dorm often, just during Thanksgiving, Christmas, and Easter. My experience was not harmful like I have heard. Mine was positive. People were friendly and kind to us. We were treated with respect. We did what we needed to do. We learned how to fix our bed, how to clean up after ourselves, and to serve others in the kitchen.

"However, my daughter Clair's experience was a little different. When she went to Pine Springs Boarding School, she did not make it because she missed us."

> "Our mom is loving in her own way. She is always for the underdog. . . . She is strong-willed and even lived through cancer."
>
> –Clarissa and Ronette Yazzie

Clair states, "I was six and in the first grade, and I would tell my family, 'I am going to boarding school. I am going to boarding school. Yay!' I had a choice. I could stay at home and ride the bus or go to boarding school. My mom would tell me that it was not all fun, but I went anyway. It turned out that I missed my own bed, and I missed everything! I lasted three days. On the third day, I found my bus at the end of the school day. I caught my own bus home at age six. I knew which bus went by my house, and I told the bus driver that I was going home and I was riding his bus. So he took me to my house. From then on, I stayed at home and rode the bus every day. I decided that getting up at five o'clock in the morning sounded a whole lot better than living over there at the boarding school."

Marian Yazzie

Ronette and Clair spent their childhood playing in the area close to their dad's church. "On rainy days we splashed in the mud. We played Barbies. We made swings out of rope and a board. We would climb trees and make a tree house. We were always outside using our imagination." Marian felt that it was important for her daughters to have what they needed and wanted.

Marian did not live as her daughters lived. "My parents struggled through life. That is why we went to boarding school. In the summer our days were spent having to deal with the sheep. We had sheep, like about 200. We would have breakfast first, feed the dogs, and then get the sheep out. We spent the whole day with them.

"While we were out there, we would spend the time making up stuff. We climbed the rocks and made trucks out of the rocks. We played with whatever was out there. There was a school nearby, and we would take beautiful glass jars from the trash, and we would play with those things. Also, we got our made-up toys from the dump. When we climbed the mountain, we made our own toys. We made our own dolls out of sticks. We played store with aspen leaves and oak leaves as our money. They were our dollars. We made jewelry out of pine needles. We would use a sheep's jawbone as a gun. Yes, we used what we had. And our guns had teeth!"

Marian knows that both of her daughters have ambition. "They are on the right track with their lives. Even though they are in their late teens and early twenties, they are old souls at heart. My husband and I had them in our thirties. They enjoy old movies and old music. They love the jazz from the 1930s, '40s and '50s."

The girls describe their mom as stubborn and yet full of surprises. "Kind of like we are. Our mom is loving in her own way. She is always for the underdog. She stands up for people who do not want to speak for themselves or who cannot speak for themselves. She is strong-willed and even lived through cancer. In our opinion, we think she is great."

Marian Yazzie

(Back, left to right) Great-granddaughter Jenneica White, Daughter Dixie Barlow, Mother June White Hair, Daughter Deidra Boone, Daughter Raquel White Hair, (Front, left to right) Great-granddaughter Nikki White, Great-grandmother Alma White, Kayenta, Arizona

Chapter 8

The White Family

"We all had our share of responsibility and that has made us who we are today."

—June White Hair, October 10, 2010

Deidrea and her sister, Dixie, grew up in a camp with many hogans on a hill south of Kayenta, Arizona. Now in their thirties, they both live in Flagstaff with their own families, but they return to their childhood camp often to see their mother, June, and grandmother, Alma.

At young ages both girls preferred to be outside instead of indoors. The family's land turned into their playground. Deidrea explains, "We would take out the sheep and goats, the total herd, for the entire day. That meant that we too were out with them for the whole time. It was not work or a chore; we saw it as play. We did not have anyone watching over us. We had the whole day to do our thing. We would come in at night and then have more fun. We had an amazing connection to nature because we were out in it all of the time. In the city we have to worry about our children, but on the reservation we would take the sheep out to graze, and it was playtime!"

Mother June describes her daughters. "Dixie seems to be my quiet daughter, and Deidrea my lively one." She adds, "We had a horse corral that was eighty feet in diameter. The poles that held up the corral were very tall, and Deidrea loved to wear dresses. She would balance herself, and she would walk around and around the corral with her dress on. Over and over again she would do this for hours and hours. She loved to be outside."

The women have a common link to the *kinaaldá*. Sister Dixie's *kinaaldá* involved staying up all night, singing songs, and saying prayers. She declares, "You run, grind corn, and learn a lot of life lessons. You learn how to carry yourself as a woman in public, how to earn respect, how to carry on in your home, and the order your home should be in. For me it is a tradition that has been passed down from the generations, and I will have one for my daughter, even though we live in the city. I want to teach her how to live."

Deidrea's *kinaaldá* occurred on a June weekend with school almost out for the summer. Deidrea asked her mother if she could put it off until school had ended, but her mother told her that would not happen. June explained to her, "This is tradition. This is how it is supposed to be."

Deidrea adds, "I had to follow what my mother said. I had to wear Navajo jewelry to school and my traditional outfit. I wore two or three necklaces and bracelets, rings on three fingers, two sash belts and a concho belt to keep me slim, to hold my tummy in, and to mold my body to how it will be shaped throughout my life. No one else was dressed that way at school. They did not have to wear their hair in a bun like I did. I probably missed a couple of days of school. My mom was very strict about the tradition. I had my second menstruation a year later to the day, and then I was in the eighth grade, and I had to have my second ceremony. And again, I had to wear my jewelry to school and my outfit. From my *kinaaldá* I learned to be ladylike. I had to sit with good posture. I had to have a good presence about myself. When you first do your run in the morning, you go a little ways. The next day you go farther, and the following day still farther. You learn strength from doing this. You see that you are strong. I selected my aunt on my father's side, and she tied my hair and dressed me up. All the while she is doing this, she is telling me all of the dos and the don'ts of being a Navajo woman. This ceremony is for four days only, but then you realize that this is how you will be living for the rest of your life. This is forever!"

Grandmother Alma, who speaks Navajo exclusively, had her *kinaaldá* at the age of fourteen. She used the grinding stones—a *metate* and *mano*—to grind the corn. She had the ceremony twice in two months for her first menstruation and second menstruation. However, June used a corn grinder instead of the stones. "And when I ran, it was so hot. I remember running in the heat. It was a warm July. Also, I learned how to present myself as a lady, how to walk, how to sleep, how to cook, how to take care of the dishes, and how to dress. All of these things were taught. If you chose to wear a frown or if you chose to be mean or disobedient, then that was how you would be when you grew up."

> "You learn strength from doing this. You see that you are strong."
>
> –Deidrea Barlow

Grandmother Alma sold her first rug when she was twelve for six dollars. "That bought a lot back then. She was probably the richest girl in Dinnehotso, Arizona." June adds, "My mom, age eighty-four, has been weaving her whole life. As she gets older, she can't do certain things. She doesn't work the stove very well, and we told her then, enough of that. We will do things for you. And she answers back that we could do things for her, but we would not take away her weaving!"

June attended school when she was seven. At home she was responsible for taking care of her younger brothers and sisters. "I was like a nanny. But then the Bureau of Indian Affairs

Alma White

people came for me. They asked why I wasn't in school, and my mom told them that I was the babysitter. I was to take care of the kids while she would herd sheep. My mom told them, 'Right now, I have no means of getting her to school, but I promise that she will go.' Then my mom put her thumbprint on a piece of paper stating that I would go to school. That fall, she took me to school in a wagon. I was lucky because my aunt lived in town, and we stayed with her and would walk to school. My childhood was different from my mother's. I was raised with both parents, and she was not. I was lucky."

June continues, "My mother taught us how to keep up a home, how to cook, and how to be a woman. Then we would go outside, and my dad would say, 'You need to saddle up, and get the cattle, or cut wood, or haul water.'" June continues, "We always had lots of work to do. In the summer when we would wake up, we had to fix our bedding, wash dishes, and take the sheep out before it got too hot. We would bring them back in mid-morning, so they could feed the young ones. Then in the late afternoon, we would take them out again and bring them back at dusk. You had to make sure that the horses were fed too.

"During lambing season you are so tired, and you would only have time to eat one meal a day. You were out at the corral helping with the newborn lambs. My parents had from 300 to 400 head. When we lamb, the sheep have to know their own babies. You have to make sure that none of the sheep are stuck in the corner and can't find their lambs. You have to get the lambs fed. It is a lot of work. I remember my mom telling me to make sure that my younger brothers and sisters had dry diapers and to check the sheep every now and then. It was too much! We all had our share of responsibility and that has made us who we are today." June explains, "There were eleven children and one stepdaughter in our family."

Deidrea describes her mom as a "good mother. She is someone who has grown very smart. She is a loving mother. She is the one who has spoken the most in her Native language. Most things that roll off of her tongue are in Navajo. When I went to preschool, I had to learn English. My Navajo has diminished a lot. The one thing I would like to leave

(Left to right) Raquel White Hair, Jenneica White, Nikki White

my children is my Native language and culture. I wish I knew how to run a *kinaaldá* and to know why you do what you do. Even simple prayers, I wish I knew. When you pray, you have to know about the four sacred mountains and about the corn pollen. My mom has always taught us, and now I don't remember because I don't use it."

Dixie declares, "My mom wanted us to be considerate of others. You should give everybody a chance to be his or her own person. You have to be respectful to everyone, and my mother was the best example of that. I could not have had a better role model. I would just watch her and learn from her. My mom did not want us to be anything but successful with life and to make her proud. My mom would describe me as intellectually, physically, and mentally strong. I got all of this from her.

"I grew up the same as my mom, in a home with no modern utilities. We spoke Navajo and English. It was more the same than different. But the way my mom raised me and the way I am bringing up my children is different. I speak both Navajo and English, but my children speak a little Navajo, and they are fluent in English. Living in the city, now we have electricity and running water. Our ways of living are unlike each other. My children have to take a field trip to go into nature, where I grew up with it. They do not have this kind of exposure to the Navajo culture and environment. It is the same for my sister's children too. We are close to nature and the Navajo way, but our kids live in the city and cannot be out in the country, which makes us sad."

2021

June White Hair said her mother, Alma, "is still with us and by the grace of the creator, she'll reach 100 years this fall! My youngest daughter has finished high school and is looking to join the workforce in the medical profession upon finishing nursing school. I'm still with my employer at the schools, looking to take the next stage in life and retire from my eight-to-five job after forty years!" Daughter Dixie lives and works in Flagstaff, Arizona, and Deidrea in Sedona, Arizona.

(Back, left to right) Daughter Gayla Montano, Daughter Melanie D. Montano, Daughter Alicia Montano, (Front) Grandmother Cynthia Montano, Granddaughter Aiden Montano, Flagstaff, Arizona

Chapter 9

The Montano Family

"When Gayla goes out and prays, it creates balance and peace for her."

—Cynthia Montano, June 29, 2009

Cynthia Montano grew up in Tsaile, Arizona, on the Navajo Reservation. Her mother worked outside the home, but Cynthia was fortunate to spend time with her grandmother, who was a medicine woman. "I remember my grandmother gathering different types of herbs for ceremonies. She taught me how to tie my hair in a bundle, and she showed me how to use the old grinding stones for cornmeal."

Even though Cynthia's grandmother was traditional, her own mother forbade Cynthia from speaking the Navajo language. "She wanted this so we would be able to succeed. It was about the assimilation. We had to only speak English, and we never learned Navajo. Our relatives would tease us when we would go and visit because they spoke only Navajo. We would try Navajo, but it would not come out right. They would laugh at us. So we just didn't speak. We were silent."

When Cynthia was older, she married Gibson Montano. Now married for twenty-seven years, Gibson first saw Cynthia in a store and told a friend, "She is going to be my wife someday." Three months later they were married.

"My husband said that I could either go to school or have kids. I chose to have kids." Then Cynthia and Gibson decided to leave Tsaile, Arizona, and began moving with their children around the country. "We lived in Colorado and California in the white society. But a major turning point was when one day we were visiting the reservation, and our children said, 'Oh Mom, Daddy, look at those Indians.' At that moment we knew we needed to move back to Tsaile and have our children live the Navajo way. We knew we had to take them back to where we came from. That was where we were meant to be.

"We built our home, a hogan, using boards to make the eight sides. It was an adventure for the kids. We lived in a tent while we were constructing the hogan. It was wonderful to finally move into our home." The family lived in their hogan for many years. Cynthia and Gibson were both silversmiths, and Gibson was also a part-time auto mechanic. It was important for Cynthia to be at home with her children as much as possible. Being a silversmith enabled her to do this. "My husband taught me how to make jewelry. Then I learned to do my own designs. By making jewelry, I could be close to my children. They often helped me buff the silver and work with the tools."

"My parents were very involved in our lives," states daughter Gayla. "They would even show up at school. They really protected us. I was always very close to my sisters and brother. We would play and go to school together. It was wonderful living in Tsaile. We worked very hard in school because we knew we were going to go on to college." Eventually all four children were in college in Flagstaff and working toward becoming the professionals their parents wanted them to be.

One October day, on Gibson's birthday, the children wanted their parents to come to Flagstaff to celebrate. But the trip did not go well. Gibson had purchased a new motor cycle, which broke down while he was riding to Flagstaff. After getting the motorcycle

Gayla Montano and Cynthia Montano

fixed, they spent a few days in Flagstaff, but the parents had an uneasy feeling that they needed to return to their home in Tsaile. Riding into the Tsaile area, they approached their hogan and noticed a tunnel of white smoke in the sky. Then they saw pieces of their furniture and appliances had been strung along the road. Their puzzlement turned into fear. Soon they found the hogan that they built engulfed in flames. All they could see was the roof burning and the walls collapsing.

Gayla exclaimed, "My mom fell apart. Even our dog, chained to the doghouse, had been knifed to death and burned. No one called for help or reported that our house was on fire. The neighbors could see the smoke. This was so painful for my mom and dad because they had helped many of their neighbors over the years. Much of what my parents had worked for had turned to ashes."

Even now, a few years later, the family spoke of the fire with tears in their eyes. It was such a great loss; their traditional clothing, all their special items from their childhood, even the tree in which they would play for hours . . . all gone. Gayla described it as total devastation. "I had never seen my dad cry until our home burned," she added. They never found out who started the fire or why it was done.

Feeling hopeless and lost, Cynthia and Gibson moved to Flagstaff, where they were able to find jobs. Living there and adjusting was difficult. The family still mourned. At times the grief seemed too difficult to bear. At least Gibson and Cynthia could be closer to their children by living in Flagstaff, and they all dealt with their heartache by practicing their Navajo traditions.

The Montano family seeks to keep their traditions alive. One ceremony, known as the Blessingway, offers prayers. Gayla's family gave her this ceremony instead of a *kinaaldá*. "When Gayla had her Blessingway," states Cynthia, "it was her introduction into womanhood. We don't do a traditional *kinaaldá* because it is a lot of money. We say our prayers for the Blessingway and bless Gayla. When Gayla goes out and prays, it creates balance and peace for her. But the prayers are not just done for her. You can't see things at eye level. You have to go beyond that. You are praying for your extended family too, and many more. You have to think about our troops and all of the other people. You ask for healing for all.

Gayla Montano

"You don't just pick a date and plan for the Blessingway. It just kind of happens," continues Cynthia. "You find yourself buying material and deer hide. You find that a medicine man is available. Then it is time. We have songs, and the songs go with the season in which the young woman is born."

"Children take on the personality of the season," adds Gayla. "If you are born in the winter, you are a quiet person as if you are hibernating. In the spring you are awake like newly growing flowers. You are a social person. In summer you are kind of moody like the weather because there are the monsoons. We have the sunshine in the morning and the rain in the afternoon. During the fall, the harvest time, you are known as a 'go-getter.' You make things happen."

Cynthia compares Gayla's birth in the fall to a "fireball." "Oh my gosh, she came so fast when she was born! And her middle name is Dawn because she was born during the dawn. If she doesn't like something, she gets upset and lets it be known. One day the school bus driver came up and honked for her to come out. She ran outside and put her hands on her hips and said, 'That is so rude! You come to the door if you need me! I am eating my cereal!' The name 'Fireball' fits her."

"She was a fast learner," adds Cynthia. "She went to preschool for just a week, and then the teacher called for a conference. Gayla already knew how to read and write, and she knew all of her colors. She started to make the other children feel inferior. Because she shared what she knew, she expected the other children to share what they knew. Her teacher told me to keep her at home and to keep doing what we were doing with her. So we did. Another time when Gayla was young, we were having a party, and she handled building the fire and preparing all the food. She even butchered the sheep and made the fry bread.

"As far as life goes, I tell Gayla and all of my children that it is all about what you put into it. It is about what you give to life. We told our daughters that they have two strikes against them. One is being female and the other is being Native American. Don't live with those strikes. Be prideful for who you are."

Gayla adds, "My parents said that they wanted to give us a good foundation by having a mom and a dad at home. My dad was responsible for teaching us the creation stories. My mom taught us about grinding corn and tying our hair in a bundle."

> "There are times when you are a mother that you go without for your kids."
> –Cynthia Montano

Cynthia reflects, "My childhood was much different than my daughters'. I grew up with alcoholics. My relatives were alcoholics. It was hard being around them. We would not allow them to come and see our children if they had been drinking."

"My parents made sacrifices for us," states Gayla. "It was understood that we would go to college. College was not optional. We were to go because they wanted us to be professionals. Anything we had to do, it had to be done professionally. My grandfather said that his grandchildren were going to be very important people. They would do great things. We as children did not understand why my grandfather was saying these things. Now that we are older, we understand what he was thinking. My parents have helped us make our lives much easier. My mother is a very compassionate person. She puts us before herself. She is giving to all of us."

"There are not words that work that describe how I feel about my children," says Cynthia with tears rolling down her face. "There are times when you are a mother that you go without for your kids, so they will make it. That is what I did."

(Back, left to right) Daughter Lisa Mann Adams, Daughter Mindy Nez, Daughter Lolita Paddock, (Front) Mother Jean H. Mann, Cameron, Arizona

Chapter 10

The Mann Family

"My mother usually prays for everybody. She asks for everyone to have a good life and to prosper. Her prayers are almost like poems or songs."

—Mindy Nez, August 1, 2010

Close to Arizona Highway 89 North, the Mann family resided in a reservation community called Cameron. Lolita Mann Paddock and her seven sisters and four brothers grew up in the framed house where her mother, Jean, still lives today. Because the family's home was situated close to the road, they did not own a camp with grazing sheep like other Navajos. Daughter Lolita explains, "Since we lived by the street, we were not the red, rosy-faced Navajos who herded sheep in the pastures that you hear about.

"When we were young, we kids earned money by living close to the highway. It was all about tourism for us. We used tourism as money-making when we were growing up. This

Jean H. Mann

all happened from 1960 to 1965. Even though some of us were girls, we would dress up like boys with horsehair braids and a loincloth. We had not developed yet. We would dance on the side of the road. Other girls would dress in long skirts and sash belts, and we would all sit out there for photos. After the tourists would take our picture, we would go up to them and say, 'Money, money, money for the picture.' They would always give us some. It was hot out in the sun, and we would really bake in the summertime. By the road we were hoop dancers. It was an art. The tourists would watch us. But to tell you the truth, we felt like roadside urchins. In the evening we would get all of these coins from the white people and bring them back to our house and count them.

"Other Cameron families did the same. Our neighbors were early risers, but we would stay out late. We weren't the early-riser type. It was all about the competition. As long as Mother was happy with our money, that was all that mattered."

Lolita loves to talk about her mom's early life. "My mother, Jean, was born across the road in between Shadow Mountain. White people were making a movie at the time. The movie was about white men and Indians. My mom didn't remember the name of the movie, but she was born during the moviemaking, and then she was raised in the Cameron area."

During the 1950s, Mother Jean, who speaks Navajo and English, attended Tuba City Boarding School in Tuba City, Arizona. Adding to the story, Jean explains, "My family would take us to school in the wagon all the way to Tuba City. We would spend the night a little beyond Shadow Mountain and make it to the boarding school the next day. Sometimes our parents would take us to school, and the school would be full, so we would not go to school that year. My mom kept us at home. Another time the school was full, and my mother decided to keep us home for that year and the next year. I only had three years of school at Tuba City. I was really mad because I wanted to go more. Then I got to go to school in Oregon and live with a family. I met my husband there. He saw me and said that he wanted to marry me. He told me that he was going to get me. I brought him back to the reservation, and he worked in the uranium mines for a while."

Jean reveals, "Then I had my very first baby, and I named her Lisa. But when my own mom saw the baby, she wanted her too, and took her away from me. I remember my own mom saying to me after giving birth, 'I am going to keep this baby cause we cannot have any more kids. You will have plenty more kids, so we will take this one.' My mother lived close to us, so I did not feel as if I had really given my baby away. Instead it was like this baby Lisa had four parents."

Now in her fifties, Lisa adds, "I was raised by my grandmother. I was raised in her hogan. I had to haul water and firewood. We used cheesecloth to filter the water. I did not speak a word of English. My grandmother did not want to put me in school. So the school officials came and had a talk with Grandma! They said, 'Come to school or else!' My grandma said that once you have been put in school, you would come home and not follow what you were supposed to do. But I went to school anyway."

> "You might think this is kind of odd, but I did not want my daughters to weave. I have eight daughters and none of them know how to weave."
>
> –Jean H. Mann

Unlike her own mother, Jean felt pleased that her children went to school. "I was really glad for them. They needed to be in school and to finish school. I wanted my daughters to work here and work there and to find a good job. I wanted them to be able to look in the paper and find a job. I told them to earn the higher money. Go for the top positions. They were to go on and on and up and up."

Lolita adds, “We all went to boarding school. When we went, none of us spoke English. I did not learn English until I was eleven. I had several years of being silent. Since my first language was Navajo, I did not know what to say. In the fifth grade I started speaking and reading English, and I never stopped. I really love to read.

“My sister Mindy and I got to live with Mormon families when we were in high school. The Mormon Church really influenced us. My sister Lisa went to live with a Mormon family when she was in the fifth grade. She was interested in that program. She was even baptized into the Mormon Church. She wanted to get away from the army-type treatment of the boarding school. The boarding school was really rigid.”

Describing where her family had lived, Lolita explains, “With my mom and dad we first lived in a canvas tent, and then my father built us a crude shack. That one burned down. Then my father built our house, the one we grew up in, and the one my mom lives in now. We did not live out in the fields on the reservation. We lived in Cameron. My parents were laborers. My dad became a carpenter. My mother worked as a maid at Buck Rodgers Trading Post. There was an old motel there too. Now it is called Speedy’s Gas Station.”

Jean was also a well-known weaver in the Cameron area. She had the opportunity to demonstrate her craft at the Grand Canyon. “One time I found out that there was a job in the Grand Canyon, and the people at the Grand Canyon wanted to know if I wanted it. So I asked my daughters, because I never worked away from home before. They all said to go ahead and take the job. We will take care of the younger kids in the family. So at the Grand Canyon these people had me living in an apartment that was already paid for. I spoke only Navajo, but I was able to pick up English over time.”

Daughter Lolita continues, “Either working as a maid or as a weaver is how I saw my mom. Besides the Grand Canyon, she would weave rugs for the Natural History Association. She

(Standing) Lolita Paddock and (Seated) Jean H. Mann holding her photograph

was part of a living-history program. She demonstrated the carding and the spinning of the wool. People watched her set up the yarn for the loom. They would sit around and observe her do all of the parts of weaving, and her rugs were worth a lot of money."

Jean adds a surprising statement, "You might think this is kind of odd, but I did not want my daughters to weave. I have eight daughters and none of them know how to weave. It is a hardship to weave all the time and to raise a family. I had to work hard and earn my way. I wanted them to be in school and finish their education."

Daughter Mindy says, "My mom wove her last rug last spring, and my own daughter bought it. My mom is now seventy-seven years old. She had to stop weaving because she has Parkinson's disease. I always saw my mom weaving. This is how it was when I was growing up. It makes me sad that she is not able to weave anymore."

Lolita states, "In raising us, Mom was not strict. She gave us a lot of choices. But she did tell us not to be with boys and not to smoke cigarettes. Our mom said, 'I cannot tell you not to go to dances because your grandmother and grandfather went to traditional dances.'"

Mindy continues, "My mother's personality is very calm and subtle. She has a nice aura about her. She is quiet, and we are loud. Our dad was boisterous with a lot of laughter. Mom is more reserved. She would tell us when we went out in public to keep it down, and she would tell us that she would not want to go out into public and hear that we were wild. She would have us sit in a circle and talk with each other. She would say to us that kids today are so unruly and loud, and you kids were not like that.

"We had fun with our play. We would take sticks and tie them to our legs and make stilts. Sometimes the church would give us clothes and high heels. We would wear the high heels and have races in them. It was great enjoyment. We believe you have to have balance in your life. You have to work hard, but you have to have fun too. I look at Mom as a role model for life because she always worked really hard.

"But we did have happy times. Even Mom did a lot of dancing in her day. You know, Native dancing. She used to do the two-step and the Navajo skip dance. Another thing you can really learn from our mother is that you can hear her praying at night. My mother usually prays for everybody. It is not like a religion. In the Navajo way, you talk to the whole universe like nature. She asks for everyone to live a good life and to prosper. She is usually praying for everybody. Her prayers are almost like songs or poems. And yes, she is a giving and loving person."

2021

At age eighty-seven, Jean Mann resides in a Flagstaff nursing home. Her daughter Lisa said, "Even though my mom has Parkinson's, she has her marbles about her! She is still aware. Because of the pandemic, we weren't able to visit her. Now if we want to see her, we have to make an appointment. Fortunately, our entire family remains safe from COVID."

While in Flagstaff, Lolita, a specialist in teaching the English language, worked with students. She left Flagstaff to undertake various positions working with Native students. She served as principal of a reservation boarding school, a reading specialist, and a supervisor at the Flagstaff Indian Dorm. She is proudest of her work at the dormitory. Students from Native reservations live in the dorm to attend Flagstaff High School. The tribe and federal government stopped funding the dorm because of poor financial planning. "The dorm was in shambles. A law firm in Flagstaff helped us in correcting the financial situation and allowed funding to resume. Now the dormitory is thriving."

Lolita left her job at the dorm to run a Hopi school and then moved to work in the Havasupai Indian Reservation at the bottom of the Grand Canyon. "My husband did not come with me, but in 2015, I adopted five foster kids, and they came with me." Havasupai, known for its blue-green waterfalls, was a favorite swimming pool for Lolita's foster children.

"I was the principal at the school, and I loved those students. Their lives were so hard, and you could see it in their eyes. There was a lot of alcohol and drugs used in the village. The teacher turnover rate was big, and some teachers did not feel safe. But other teachers have been there a long time and love it. For me to leave, I would fly out on a helicopter, thirty-five dollars out and thirty-five dollars in. I would see my husband on weekends because he had to work at his engineering job.

> "We believe you have to have balance in your life. You have to work hard, but you have to have fun too."
>
> –Mindy Nez

"I almost lost my husband to kidney failure, and I knew it was time to retire. He will need a kidney transplant. We have traveled to Hawaii and have rafted a river. Now, we are living in Kaibeto, Arizona, in a HUD community for elderly Navajo. I would say I am happily retired."

A few years ago, Lisa Mann Adams retired from a job in human resources at the Department of the Interior. Sister Mindy is a backcountry ranger. The five sisters in the family find joy in hiking the Arizona trails. They have completed several rim-to-rim hikes in the Grand Canyon, and the five are glad they have each other as fellow hikers.

Grandmother Rita Francisco and Mother LaShia Scharfenberger, Flagstaff, Arizona

Chapter 11

The Francisco Family

"I would go with my grandma to the cornfield and water the corn. It was always me and my grandma. I loved being with her."
—LaShia Scharfenberger, October 16, 2011

Mother Rita Francisco and her daughter LaShia Scharfenberger grew up in the wide landscapes of Greasewood, Arizona. Both women had a great deal of energy when they were young. Mother Rita was the only girl in a family of four boys. "My brothers would put me on horseback, poke the horse, and I would take off! I would play with . . . boys' toys. My brothers and I would carve guns and cars. All of our toys were homemade.

"My daughter, LaShia, like me, was busy all of the time. She hardly played with dolls. She played outdoors. You know the reservation was wide-open, and you didn't have to worry about living like you do in the urban areas. There were corrals and pets like dogs, cats, and sheep."

Both Rita and LaShia went to boarding school. LaShia was lucky that she lived close to the boarding school, and she could come home every day. On the other hand, Rita was sent to school in the fall and would return at Christmas. Rita says, "I must have been maybe six years old. My family only had a wagon. Thinking about it, though, it was fun traveling there. We could get off and run and play because the wagon would travel slowly. We lived about twelve miles from the school. So my parents took us all and left us there. I thought this was too much, but they went ahead and left us. Actually it was good that I went to the boarding school because I learned how to do chores, how to clean up, do sports, and even help out in the cafeteria. It was not so bad. In fact it was fine.

"But one thing I did not like was when I learned how to speak English. I spoke Navajo when I got there. It was hard learning English because we weren't allowed to speak our own language. Every time we would say something in Navajo, we would get punished for it. They would put soap in our mouths. They would make us sit in the corner and scrub the floors. They would really punish us. This was the early sixties, where you weren't allowed to talk Navajo. But when nobody was around, we would talk it. It was around second grade when I finally learned how to speak English. I went to a Bureau of Indian Affairs boarding school."

LaShia spoke Navajo but doesn't now. "My grandma says I spoke Navajo because I would be with her all of the time. I would go everywhere with her. I would go to functions and happenings in the community, and I would go with her and her friends. When we went to town, we would talk with her friends. Somewhere along the way, I started speaking English. I had cousins that I would play with, and I learned English from them. But Navajo is my first language. I understand Navajo, but I have a hard time speaking it. Now I speak little phrases here and there. I am not fluent. In college I took Navajo classes and can read and write it. I just can't speak it."

Rita had a difficult childhood. "We started out in a hogan and then moved to a framed house. That hogan still exists. We really did not have anything. We wished we had more,

Sariah Scharfenberger and La Shia Scharfenberger

but we didn't. It was hard work. There was a lot of working with the livestock and cornfields. We used to get sent out to the cornfields early in the morning. We would spend the whole day hoeing out there. Besides school, those were my childhood years. There was no electricity and no running water. We had to haul all of our water. We had no inside plumbing, and we had kerosene lamps. I would read by those oil lamps, and it would strain my eyes."

As a child LaShia spent time with her grandmother. Rita became a single parent because her husband left her when the children were young. Rita had to work, and so LaShia was with her grandmother. "My job with my grandma was to help clean up. My brothers would take the sheep out. I would go with my grandma to the cornfield and water the corn. It was always me and my grandma. I loved being with her."

Rita learned much about how to live from her own mother. "My mom taught me that if you are a woman, you have to present yourself in the right way. You must take care of your family. Family is number one. My mom used to say that I could not sleep in. You have to get up early in the morning and start cooking. Do what is important for your family. My mom was strict with me. I was to respect myself. I was to be strong. If you are not strong, then you won't know how to deal with life. It seems as if they knew my future. I was a single mom, and I had to care for my children. I had to be tough and handle life. It was really difficult at times, but my children made me who I am today."

Rita continues, "I wanted LaShia to be how she is right now. At age thirty-two, LaShia is educated and independent. She is doing things on her own. She went far in her education. She waited to start her family. She has two daughters, a four-year-old and a three-month-old. My family was different because my husband and I married when we were very young. Now LaShia works as a counselor, and her husband is in physical therapy school."

LaShia's children's lives will be different from LaShia's. "Since I was raised on the reservation, I had free reign about what I wanted to do. Where I could play was wide

Aviana Scharfenberger

open. If I wanted to go to the barn and be with the animals, I could do that. If I wanted to just run, I could do that. I don't see us moving back to the reservation. When my husband is done, we will go where his job takes him. My children will not have that sense of freedom or independence. We live in Flagstaff, Arizona, and my daughter will want to run outside in the front yard. I cannot let her do that. It is not safe. I will have to watch her every minute. Everything is confined here."

LaShia continues, "I want my girls to make the right choices, and I would want them to be successful and to have an education. I do not want them to make the same mistakes I made. When I was really young, I somehow got into debt. I did not know how to save money and how to pay my credit card. Those mistakes set me back. I want my children

Aviana Scharfenberger and LaShia Scharfenberger

to be accomplished in what they choose to do. I am fearful because of the teenagers I work with. They struggle with life. How can I prevent my daughters from going that way? I don't want that for my girls. My daughters I hope will have a sense of where they came from and know how they were raised. I want them to be connected to my mother and my grandmother."

Rita adds, "I was really worried about LaShia when she was born. I had to work and could not stay home. My husband had left us. Luckily my parents helped me out. But now I get to take care of LaShia's new baby while she works. I live in Tuba City, Arizona, and come to help her during the week.

"You know, the baby just had her first laugh the other day. I made her laugh, so it is my responsibility to have a party for the baby. We believe that if we have a party for her, then she won't become selfish or greedy. When you have the party, you give away gifts, and you even give away salt so the child will not be bitter. You want them to be generous. We are having a party for her this weekend. We will invite family and friends."

LaShia explains, "We could tell that the baby was getting ready to laugh. But we would all say, 'She is not laughing for me! I am not the one!' Finally my mom was feeding her, and her clothes were wet. My mom said that she had to change the baby, and the baby started laughing. So my mom has to give the party."

LaShia and her mother are close. Rita says that her daughter is extremely responsible and is a wonderful mother to her children. LaShia describes her mother as supportive and as someone who has sacrificed a lot for her brothers and her. "Even today, as adults, she still cares for us."

Mother Elsie D. Nez and Daughter Amy N. Begay, Rock Point, Arizona

Chapter 12

The Nez Family

"Herding sheep on horseback, she would be pregnant, carrying one baby in front on her lap, with three babies tied to her back, all wrapped up in a flour sack to keep them safe."

—Amy Begay about Elsie Nez, July 19, 2009

Amy Begay's mother, Elsie D. Nez, is a well-known weaver in the Rock Point, Arizona, area. Amy translates her mother's weaving and life stories as Elsie sits close by. "As a young child, my mother, Elsie, would weave rugs. Her siblings would 'run off' to school, and she had to stay behind and weave. She did not mind because it was a way for her to make an income. When my grandmother, her mom, became ill, my mom had to take over the weaving duties. She would herd sheep in the morning and come home in the afternoons to card and spin the wool. My mother's first rug was made when she was seven.

"She would spend hours weaving with my grandmother. Sometimes my mom would fall asleep while she was carding. Some of the rugs were so large that my mom and grandmother had to weave them together. When my grandmother was making the warp, my mother would stand on the other side so that Grandma could pass the yarn through. At times my grandmother would weave in triangles, and my mother had to fill in the spaces. In the afternoons my grandmother would say that it was time for her to go and cook, but my mom had to keep on weaving.

"At the age of nine, my mom wanted a pair of saddle shoes. Her family had always given her tennis shoes, and she was not happy with them. So my grandfather made her a pair of moccasins, but they were too slippery when they were wet. My grandfather told her to weave a rug and buy the kind of shoes she wanted. She did as she was told and took her rug to the trading post. She sold it immediately, and the next time the family went to town she bought herself a pair of saddle shoes that she wore with pride.

> "She had to run as far as she was able and turn around and come back to where she started."
>
> –Amy Begay

"When my mother was about thirteen, she had her *kinaaldá*. Part of the ritual was for my mother to get up early in the morning to grind corn kernels using the stones: the *metate* and the *mano*. Then she had to run as far as she was able and turn around and come back to where she started. The second, third, and fourth day, she had to grind corn kernels and run even farther, sometimes chasing boys.

"My mother was always sad about her *kinaaldá*. Usually when a girl is eleven or twelve, the family starts to collect jewelry for the girl to wear during the *kinaaldá*. But her family did not do that. They had to borrow a necklace. That is all she had. This was very painful for her. Even today, she still cries over it."

Elsie D. Nez

Amy's mother spent the next several years weaving, but when she was fifteen, Amy's parents arranged her marriage. "My mom was told that a man was coming, and there was going to be a wedding, her wedding! My mother did not want this. She did not want to be married off. But that did not seem to matter. Gifts were placed in front of her from the man's family. They placed a concho belt, a necklace, some earrings, and some money. My mom's response was still 'No!' She instructed the family to take it all back. Finally her father, my grandfather, had to step in and tell her she had to get married. He said that this is how it is done. This is what we do. She did not have a choice. Family members took the gifts. Her mother took the concho belt, her father the earrings, her brother the necklace, and the wedding followed.

"At seventeen, her first baby arrived. Then she had baby after baby after baby, eight girls and one boy. She had three other boys; two were stillborn and one died of sickness. They were all born in the hospital, and since my mother did not speak English, the nurses had to name all of the babies.

"My mom taught us herding and weaving."

–Amy N. Begay

"She had to keep weaving to get an income to help care for her babies. Also, my dad took a job with the railroad, so he was gone a lot. Herding sheep on horseback, she would be pregnant, carrying one baby in front on her lap, with three babies tied to her back, all wrapped up in a flour sack to keep them safe. Everyone was always sunburned.

"My dad built two camps for our family, a summer camp and a winter camp. We were always moving back and forth from the mesas to the valley to give the sheep good grass. During the winter, my mom was by herself a lot of the time with all of her children. Luckily my grandmother and grandfather were close by, and they would help.

Elsie D. Nez and Amy N. Begay

"Now at age seventy-six, my mom has raised her children. And she is still weaving. My sisters and I have learned much about the Navajo ways. My mom taught us herding and weaving. We attended Rock Point Community School, which was not far from our home in the valley. When we were in school, we had to live in the camp close to the school while our parents were in the winter camp up on the mesa. We did not always have enough firewood, and the house where we lived was cold. We liked going to school. It was warm there and we always had plenty of food. My mom did not have to worry about us when we were attending school." Amy adds, "When we left for school, it was hard for my mom because she had to do most of the work, and she did not have anyone around to help her.

"My childhood and my mom's childhood were very different. I did not have to work as hard as she did. My brothers, sisters, and I were all well-educated. But my mom never pushed education on us because she and my dad did not know about education. We went to school because we were supposed to.

> "I want to keep the traditions alive. I know my mom is proud of me, my brothers, and sisters."
>
> –Amy N. Begay

"We were poor, and I knew I did not want that. I wanted to make something of myself. My mom said that she wanted me to learn how to weave and to keep working with my crafts. She wanted me to be able to take care of myself. And that is what I did. She did not tell me what she wanted me to do. I just knew I was supposed to support myself. Education is important to me, and so I went to college. Today I teach students in Flagstaff about the Navajo language and culture. I want to keep the traditions alive. I know my mom is proud of me, my brothers, and sisters."

2021

Amy expressed excitement that her mom, Elsie, celebrated her eighty-eighth birthday. "My mom is still weaving but now uses store-bought yarn instead of dyeing her yarn from plants. Her health is not the best because she has diabetes and has fallen a few times, even breaking her hip. We all realized she could not live by herself." Elsie spends short periods of time with a few of her daughters and sometimes returns back to her Rock Point home, where some of her twenty-eight grandchildren care for her.

Amy and her husband, Joe, continue to preserve Navajo language and traditions. Amy teaches Navajo language and culture classes to middle school students in Flagstaff. Joe teaches Navajo language and Navajo history and government to high school students. Amy and Joe will retire in a year. "We are both looking forward to that day," Amy said, "but in the meantime, we are doing our best to give our Navajo teaching to the students."

(Back, left to right) Mother Stephanie Smith, Grandmother Kathy Powell, (Front) Daughter Melissa Gorman, Houck, Arizona

Chapter 13

The Powell Family

"It was difficult for me to live in two worlds as a child. It was hard for me to go back and forth from Cedar Rapids, Iowa, to the reservation."

—Kathy Powell, June 9, 2011

Grandmother Kathy Powell, mother Stephanie Smith, and daughter Melissa Gorman all live together in HUD/NHA government housing in Houck, Arizona, close to Interstate 40. Kathy, a secretary at Sanders Elementary School in Sanders, Arizona, on the Navajo Reservation, has been working there for a number of years.

"My childhood was very different from my daughter Stephanie's," explains Kathy. "I was born in a hogan. Stephanie was born in a hospital. My family did not have electricity and running water at that time. At age five, I went to live with foster parents in Cedar Rapids, Iowa. My biological parents thought I should leave to get a better education. They only

Kathy Powell and Stephanie Smith

wanted what they thought would be the best for me, so they agreed to let me go. It was somewhat like the Mormon Placement Program, but my foster parents were not members of the Mormon Church.

"At first I could only write to my parents, and I could not call them because they did not have electricity. My foster parents helped my parents to have a framed house built on our land. My parents were able to get electricity and have a telephone installed, so I was able to call my parents and speak to them from Iowa. They were one of the first people in our area to have a framed house and electricity.

"I lived with my foster family in Cedar Rapids for eleven months out of the year. During the summer I was able to come back to Houck to visit and stay with my parents and the rest of my family for about a month. It was difficult for me to live in two worlds as a child. It was hard for me to go back and forth from Cedar Rapids, Iowa, to the reservation. Just as I would be getting used to being home on the Navajo Reservation, it was time to go back to Iowa for school.

> "My foster parents were good to me. I believe I learned a lot of things from them."
>
> –Kathy Powell

"Because I lived in Iowa from such an early age, I lost a lot of my Navajo language. I had to repeat kindergarten so that I could learn English. Being away from the Navajo language and having no one to talk to, I forgot most of it. I am not a fluent Navajo speaker, and I regret that part of my life. Because of this and the fact that Stephanie and my other children were not exposed to Navajo on a daily basis, they speak very little of it and cannot carry on a conversation. However, they would hear their grandmother and grandfather and other family members speak Navajo.

Kathy Powell, Melissa Gorman, Stephanie Smith

"I would miss my parents and family whenever I would leave to go back to Iowa, but as the school year progressed, I would get back into my daily routines and just wait until summer would come again. My foster parents were good to me. I believe I learned a lot of things from them, and I appreciate the fact that they took me in and provided for me.

"I attended kindergarten through fifth grade in Iowa. One of my brothers was living in Clinton, Iowa, and one of my sisters was also living in Cedar Rapids. We were able to see each other on different occasions. My brother eventually moved to Cedar Rapids from Clinton also. I came from a large family with nine siblings, while Stephanie has three brothers.

“While in Iowa, my brother, sister, and I received a call saying that our mother was sick, so we came back to Houck. My mother was diagnosed with a brain tumor and was to be taken to Albuquerque to have surgery. At that time she was still into the traditional ways and her half-sister had a four-day traditional ceremony for her. She got well and never had surgery. She became a Christian many years later, and we would go to church with her at the Assembly of God across the freeway from our house. She set a good example for us, and we could see the changes in her life. I believe in God, and I think he healed her because he had plans for her to guide us into becoming Christians also. I believe he still performs miracles today.

“My kids and I consider ourselves to be Christian, and we do not do any of the traditional ceremonies such as the *kinaaldá*. I did not have one because I was away from the reservation, and I did not have one for Stephanie. However, I do like the taste of the Navajo cake that is made during the *kinaaldá*. We were taught not to combine Christian ways with traditional ways.

“When Stephanie was born, there were not many babies in my family, so she received a lot of attention. She was always being carried around, and she would go to her relatives’ houses. Stephanie had a lot of energy and was running all of the time. Someone commented she would be a track star someday because she liked to run, but that never happened.

“Stephanie attended Navajo Nation Head Start and went to elementary, middle school, and part of high school in Sanders, Arizona. She graduated from St. Johns High School in St. Johns, Arizona. Stephanie has grown into a beautiful young woman and is now raising her daughter Melissa in much the same way she herself was raised. I have been able to raise my children in some of the ways I was brought up, and I truly believe they have grown to be upstanding adults.”

Mother Lisa Puente and Grandmother Edith Puente, Sanders, Arizona

Chapter 14

The Puente Family

"My life was different than my daughter Lisa's. I did not have the necessities, and I learned not to take life and things for granted. I wanted to make my kids' lives different."

—Edith Puente, June 7, 2011

In the early 1950s, Edith Puente's mother really wanted to go to school, but her mother, Edith's grandmother, told her she could not go. "My mom had a rough childhood, but it made her stronger. My mom's brothers and sisters could go to school, but only my mom had to stay home and help her mother. Sometimes my mother would run away from home and try to go to the boarding school. But she did not speak English and would always return home. It made her very sad not to have an education."

Edith adds, "Because my mom could not read or write, she really wanted me to attend school. When I was older, I tried to teach my mom how to read. She would not always

Edith Puente and Lisa Puente

understand what she was reading. She learned just a few words, like 'bye-bye.' I had to always translate for her when we would go shopping in town."

During the 1970s, when Edith went to school, it did not turn out well. She says that one of the most painful times in her life was when she attended boarding school. "The school was OK; it was the dorm that wasn't. I was six years old when I went to school. I really missed my mom, and I did not get to go home. The dorm ladies pinched my ears and shaved my head because of lice. My hair was really long, and they cut it really short. My mom was very, very upset when she saw me. My parents were not educated. They were poor, and so the dorm ladies would treat me badly because I did not have money. I did not have a lot of the things that other kids had."

Life improved for Edith when she went to school in Utah. "I was in the Mormon Placement Program. Because we were living in poverty, I could go and live with a Mormon family. So I was placed with a family and attended school from ninth grade to twelfth grade. I was so scared when I first went there. I did not know how to live with white people. I was speaking a lot of Navajo when I went to Utah. Living there, I learned English. I was with a good family. The mother was a homemaker. She made homemade bread. She had a garden. I learned how to can and about food storage. I used to read to my foster brother and sisters. I think that is why my own kids learned to read at such an early age. It is because I read to them.

"My life has been different than my daughter Lisa's. I did not have the necessities, and I learned not to take life and things for granted. I wanted to make my kids' lives different. Now, my husband works in construction, so we do not have to worry too much. We settled in Sanders, Arizona, and we are doing OK there."

When Lisa went to school, Edith felt fear about how her daughter would fit in. "Lisa was my first child to go to school. I was nervous about how she would be treated. I think that is because of what happened to me at the boarding school. That was an awful time for me, and so I wanted Lisa to have a different experience. I did not want her to go through what I went through."

Lisa, a thirty-year-old, fifth-grade teacher who has her own young daughter, knew Edith would be involved in her own children's schooling. "I understood my mom would be there at my school. She was always supportive and concerned. I would look up in class, and there she'd be. She really cared a lot about what I did. I felt really secure."

When it came time for their *kinaaldás*, both Edith and Lisa had one. Edith said that her mom told her, "One day you will become a woman. You will know when it is your time. When my period came, my mom said that we were going to go and tell my grandma. My mom did not wait a day. We got the medicine man and got everything together. My whole family was involved. I made it the same for Lisa when she had hers. To her, it seemed foreign. She just listened and followed what her aunts told her to do. And when it is my granddaughter Autumn's time, she will have one too."

> "Running helps me keep my life in balance spiritually, mentally, and physically. It clears my mind and keeps me alert."
>
> –Edith Puente

One aspect of Edith's life that makes Lisa proud is that her mom loves to run. At age fifty, Edith still competes. Edith states, "Running helps me keep my life in balance spiritually, mentally, and physically. It clears my mind and keeps me alert. I enjoy the run. I look at the cedar trees, and I am at peace. The whole scenery makes me want to sprint harder, and it makes me feel healthy. The hills and the trees are my training ground. I run with the wind, the snow, and the rain. I have participated in more than a dozen marathons. Many members of our tribe are becoming diabetic. My mom was diabetic, and so I want to run

Lisa Puente and Autumn Siyuja

away from diabetes. I think I am giving my example to my own kids. Each one of my kids is active. We go for runs and walks. I am always looking in the *Navajo Times* for the next 5K or 10K. I set my calendar for the next race."

> "She already is a success in life, and I know she will continue to be."
>
> –Edith Puente

Edith adds, "Lisa will be a good role model for her child. Of course she exercises, but she will also be very giving, loving, and creative. She is a quiet person who always wants to do her best. I am proud of her. She already is a success in life, and I know she will continue to be."

2021

Lisa Puente found her true calling in educating Native American adults. She shared, "Currently, I'm thirty-nine years old and will be turning forty years old on April 23. I believe at the time of the interview I was engaged to Autumn's dad, Lanny Siyuja. We got married on June 25, 2011. This June we will be celebrating our tenth wedding anniversary. Autumn is eleven years old now and will be twelve years old in November. She's in the fifth grade.

"I'm still teaching and have taught in multiple schools since Sanders Elementary. I've transitioned to teaching Adult Basic Education and GED prep classes for the Hualapai Education and Training Center in Peach Springs, Arizona. I work for the Hualapai Tribe, which is where my husband descends from. I love it!

"I think I've found my calling because there's such a need for this unique population of adult learners. So far, the program I lead has thirty GED graduates, which is a huge accomplishment for this rural area. The high school graduation and dropout rate is nearly 75 percent, and there were no local programs to help guide these adult-aged students.

"Since starting my employment here three years ago, I yearned to become a better adult education instructor and adapt my skills to the many needs of the community. This propelled me to pursue an advanced degree. I started my master's program in January 2020 and finished in December 2020.

"I can't believe I finished this program in one year and during a pandemic. I think working full-time from home and being a full-time student allowed me to focus on my studies, therefore allowing me to keep my mind on positive things I can control rather than what was going on worldwide and the pandemic.

"It was very challenging, but I did it. So, I graduated with a Master of Education in Educational Technology with an emphasis in Adult Learning and Training.

"My mother is still teaching and is currently teaching fourth grade in Pine Springs, Arizona, located near Sanders, Arizona. She had to overcome the challenges most educators faced during the pandemic as well. I think with my educational technology background, we both leaned on each other for support and guidance. My mom tested positive for COVID-19 in December 2020 and has since recovered. My dad, brother, and brother-in-law also tested positive during the pandemic. So this was also hard to cope with because you think of the worst-case scenario. All have recovered and are doing well."

Edith also has three grandchildren. Lisa added, "I think it's neat that my mom has two granddaughters, one named Autumn and the other Summer."

Granddaughter Margaret Marie Wauneka Goodwin, Grandmother Marie J. Nez, Mother Mable Wauneka Goodwin, Tuba City, Arizona

Chapter 15

The Wauneka Nez Family

"The Navajo traditions make us strong and let us know who we are. Unfortunately, I skipped a beat with the Navajo traditions. I did not participate much in the traditional life. That makes me sad."

—Mable Wauneka Goodwin, October 9, 2010

Grandmother Marie J. Nez is proud of her family's past. "My family has a history," she explains. "My great-great-grandmother was part of The Long Walk. She was taken to Fort Sumner in New Mexico. My great-great-grandfather, who was a soldier during the Civil War, was supposed to watch over these Navajos. He was Irish. His last name was Damon. He noticed my great-great-grandmother who was Navajo, and they got together and got married. Then they ended up having all of these children. If you go to the Fort Defiance, Arizona, area, you will find all of the people whose last name is Damon."

Marie proudly adds, "We are also related to Annie Wauneka. She was married to my grandfather's brother. She was a famous Navajo lady who talked with Navajos about their health. She helped them get better water on the reservation and helped to fight tuberculosis. She even received an award from President Lyndon Johnson. I believe it was the Presidential Medal of Freedom. This happened in 1963.

"Education is really important to us. My parents had a lot of sheep, but they would not let us stay home and help. We had to be in school. We would come home for the weekends, so they would pick us up on Friday, but as soon as Sunday afternoon rolled around, they would haul us back in the wagon to the boarding school in Tuba City. We could not miss one day of school. We were all to have jobs when we grew up. There was to be no welfare. These days kids are more wild. Parents need to teach their children the value of life. Being with education makes you more powerful."

Marie continues, "When I first went to school, it was lonely, and then I got used to it. I was depressed. Navajo was my first language. When I went to boarding school, they told us not to speak Navajo. It had to be all in English. I was six years old. We had Hopis at the school, and they had to speak English too. They did teach us a lot, like how to be self-sufficient. I can remember that every day they would herd us into the sewing room, and we used to darn and sew. Not with a sewing machine but by hand. We learned in cooking how to put coal in the stove. That is how we did our baking. We used to get up early, like around six o'clock, and dress for the day. We all had chores to do. That was our basic life. Take care of yourself and where you sleep. We had to work hard at the boarding school.

"My childhood was different from my daughter Mable's. I grew up in Low Mountain. Mable grew up in Tuba City. My mom died when I was a toddler. I had an infant sister too. Then my dad had an arranged marriage to a mean woman. Looking back, she really wasn't very smart. I think she had a low IQ. She would just react with only her emotions. Luckily my siblings took care of my little sister and me.

"In the summertime at our place we had to get up early and herd sheep, help with the cooking, and work in the fields. We had to hoe the cornfields. That is what I enjoyed doing the most.

"Also, we would herd the sheep in the morning, and bring them back in the afternoon, and let them out again in the evening. We had a lot of fun playing while the sheep were grazing. If you were at the hogan, you had to prepare food for the people who were herding the sheep. We had to haul water and wood for the woodstove. We had to clean up the hogan. We were always busy. We could never sleep during the day. You sleep your life away, and then you get nothing done. That is what we were taught.

"One time when we were herding, we found a stink bug, and we started to play with it. The sheep would walk really slow, but when we looked up, we found that they were gone. We had lost the sheep! We didn't know where to go. Then we saw smoke. It must have been coming from a nearby camp. We had lost the sheep, but luckily the sheepdogs knew where to take them. We walked towards the smoke and could see the house. The sheep were found close to there. We had lost the whole herd for a while. We were not the best sheepherders."

Mable says, "My mother is strong, and she is always there for me. She always, always preached to us to never depend on a man. 'Get educated. He may die on you! He may leave you! He may become disabled! It is up to you to provide for your family.' That was repeated and repeated to me. That is why I am a teacher today. I tell my own daughter the same. I passed this down to her. My brother is the same way. She told him never to depend on a woman. My brother is able to care for the house and his children if something were to happen to his wife."

Mable Wauneka Goodwin, Marie J. Nez, Margaret Marie Wauneka Goodwin

At Marie's *kinaaldá*, her corn cake was her favorite part. "I really loved the corn cake, even though I could not eat any of it at my own *kinaaldá*. To make the corn even sweeter, we would have the children put the sweet corn in their mouths and then spit it in the batter. It wasn't a big spit! It was a little spit because spit makes it sweeter. Only the young people would do it. Today we have sugar, and the *kinaaldá* has been modernized."

Navajo traditions have become significant to Mable as an adult, but when she was young they were not as important. Mable's daughter had a *kinaaldá*, but Mable did not. She explains, "My daughter had a *kinaaldá*, but I didn't want one because that was just like announcing that you got your period! I was totally against it. But when my daughter's time came around, I told her that she needed to have one. It is part of our tradition and our heritage, and it is a ceremony so that you can grow into womanhood; it makes you stronger. It causes you to think about where you came from. I wanted her to have that experience."

Margaret, age fourteen, adds, "The first day of my *kinaaldá*, I sat in a hogan and the medicine man and his wife came over. They were scolding me for not sitting correctly. I told them that I was so sorry, and they told me not to be sorry. They said that I was just never to do that again. Then I had to run and run. Someone was to run and follow me. But no one ran after me except my cousin. He ran after me all of that week, and no one else did. They increased the running distance every day. First by a half a mile and then three-quarters of a mile, and they stretched it out even more. The last run counted the most because everyone came and watched me. I stayed up all night, and they made me run at about four o'clock in the morning! After the run, they dunked my head in cold water and washed my hair in yucca. Then I ran to my great-grandma's house, and I had a huge line of people behind me. They were not allowed to pass me. They said that I would look old if they passed me. This is all about endurance and becoming stronger. Now I can carry on."

Margaret continues, "Everyone comes and donates baskets full of stuff to give to the helpers of the *kinaaldá*. We made the cake using ground cornmeal. I did a lot of grinding every day that whole week. We added raisins and wheat germ to the batter. We mixed it all up in huge tubs. They were so heavy that two men had to lift them. We had stirring spoons for each tub. There were seven tubs in all. You want the batter to be mushy, and when you pour it, it settles down. I had to sew cornhusks together, and they acted like the liner for the cake.

"We had to bake the cakes in the ground. We dug a five-by-five big hole. They put tin foil in the hole and the cornhusk liners. Then I had to bless it with corn pollen. The cake bakes overnight. A fire was built four days earlier, and we had to keep it going all that time because that is where you will bake the cake. Somebody always had to tend the fire. For the fire we wanted these big stumps. Then we put the hot ash from the stumps on top of the cake. There was singing and praying all night long. I have to behave as a young lady. They kept telling me to wake up. I knew this was the one thing that I had to get right. In the morning after the run, everybody got to eat the cake. They said it was the best cake ever, even though I was not allowed to eat any of the cake. It was a big cake, and everyone got big pieces."

Mable adds, "The Navajo traditions make us strong and let us know who we are. Unfortunately, I skipped a beat with the Navajo traditions. I did not participate much in the traditional life. That makes me sad now. I had a great learning curve when it came to my own daughter's *kinaaldá*. My grandfather was a medicine man, and he never told me to be involved. This is not what I want for my daughter Margaret. I want her to know the traditions and be a strong Navajo. I want to be like my mother, Marie, who is a strong Navajo woman and who is always there for me."

2021

Mable Wauneka Goodwin taught Diné students at Leupp Public School, part of the Flagstaff Unified School District, located in Leupp, Arizona, on the Navajo Nation. Now, as her career comes to an end, she has returned to Leupp. "I started with Natives, and

Marie J. Nez and Mable Wauneka Goodwin

I will finish with Natives." Mable, teaching third graders, must do it remotely even though the rest of the Flagstaff Unified School District has returned to in-person instruction. Navajo President Jonathan Nez extended a stay-at-home order for the Navajo Nation to decrease the spread of new variants. "My husband and I are COVID-19 survivors. I ended up with a bad sinus infection, and my husband had no symptoms.

"My daughter Margaret is married to her high school sweetheart, and they have two boys. Margaret was a success in high school and was second in command in ROTC. Currently, she works for the Arizona Attorney General's Office in Flagstaff."

Mable's mom, Marie, and her dad live near Tuba City at their ranch. "They are in their eighties and are slowly getting around."

Daughter Jolene N. Yazzie and Mother Laura Lee Yazzie, Lupton, Arizona

Chapter 16

The Yazzie Family

"Your integrity and your character come from the long line of your ancestors. My great-grandmother, my grandmother, my mom, they all passed them along."

—Laura Lee Yazzie, June 8, 2011

Fifty-eight-year-old Laura Lee Yazzie has a large family and is manager of Lupton Chapter House Community Center in Lupton, Arizona, on the Navajo Reservation. She has two daughters. Laura Lee describes one as aggressive and talkative, just like her father. The other daughter, Jolene, age thirty-two, is a quiet, private person like Laura Lee. Laura Lee adds, "But when Jolene was a child, that was not the case. She always got into mischief and would follow her brothers around all of the time. She wanted to do what they did. Stealing lumber from her dad, she would build tree houses with them. Jolene was more like a tomboy. I was always trying to dress her up in cute outfits, and she did not like that. She wanted Fridays to come because I would let her choose her clothes on that day."

Today Jolene works for a Santa Fe, New Mexico, newspaper as a graphic designer. Laura Lee says, "She loves to draw, and her older brother once gave her a challenge to draw something, and from that moment on she got really interested in drawing."

Jolene continues, "When I was ten, my brothers were really into comic books, and one of my brothers gave me a dare. He brought me a comic book, showed me a picture, and said, 'Do you think you could draw this?' So I thought, 'OK, my brother has asked me to draw, and he has never asked that before. I really want to impress him.' That is how my love of drawing started. My mom would buy me crayons, and my older sister would catch me drawing on her walls! I had a difficult time in school, especially with math and spelling. When it came to drawing, I was always comfortable with that.

"Around the age of twelve, I was to have my *kinaaldá*, but I did not want one. I was really tomboyish, and I would always hear about other girls having theirs and talking about it. It was one of these things where I was uncomfortable with myself, and I was going through this whole identity thing. It was best that I did not have one. However, my mother did have one."

Laura Lee states, "It was during the winter, and I was going to school in Holbrook, Arizona. My grandmother really emphasized the importance of having a *kinaaldá*. I decided that if I had girls, I would not put that kind of pressure on them. I did not have to worry about it because it turned out that my girls were not interested.

"When I had mine, it was really cold, and my hair was wet. Of course I had to run. I remember I had to run up to the mountain, and when I came back, my hair was all icicles. They had washed my hair that morning, and it was really, really cold. My *kinaaldá* was very important in my life because of my grandmother. She wanted me to have a *kinaaldá* because she told me it would make me into the person I am today.

"My grandmother had a strong influence on me. When I was older, I decided to look back and reflect on all of the things my grandmother taught me. I was afraid I had lost all of her teachings in my mind. But then I started writing in a journal when I was in my thirties, and it started coming back to me. At first it was one or two pages. But then I started writing and writing. So far I have twenty-two journals. I have written down what my grandmother has taught me because I want my children and grandchildren to read her stories.

> "I was afraid I had lost all of her [my grandmother's] teachings in my mind. But then I started writing in a journal when I was in my thirties, and it started coming back to me."
>
> –Laura Lee Yazzie

"In the fall, winter, and spring, I was in boarding school, but in the summer, a lot of my childhood was spent at my grandmother's house. My grandmother would get us up really early, like four-thirty or five. She had us run as far as we could, and then we would come back and do chores. If a little lamb needed to be fed, we would make its bottle and feed it. We would take the sheep out of the corral and herd them. We had fun during those times. My other cousins would come over, and we would play and have a good time. Sometimes we would ride horses. If it rained, we would play in the mud; it was really fun then. In the evening we would bring the sheep back.

"My grandmother would always cook outside. She would make the dough for fry bread and bake the potatoes in the fire. After we would eat, we would do the dishes. She would share her evening time by telling us stories. While she told us the stories, we would watch her brush her hair. Next we would wash up. Then we would go to sleep under the shade house on sheepskin or goatskin. It was comfortable so we never complained about sleeping on it.

"I was learning how to weave from my grandmother. She told me stories about the rugs. She taught me how to spin and card, and we were going to start making a rug when she passed away. It was a really emotional time because she was always there for me. My mom was there for me too, but she was also going through a really traumatic time, losing her mother. She was focusing on herself and not on me."

Laura Lee adds, "I have my grandmother's loom, and I wrote some poems about her. I wrote about how you have to leave one thread of a different color, and that it rests at the corner of the rug. She would tell me that was where the ancestor's spirits travel so they would never be caught or stranded inside of the rug. My grandmother explained it to me, and I explained it to my two daughters."

Daughter Jolene's childhood days were in some ways not the same as her mom's. "My parents would leave for work, and then I would fight with my brothers. Whatever they wanted to do, I wanted to do. But sometimes I would do my own thing. I would go off alone and climb trees and sit up on the branches. I would roam the area and hike. My imagination would go wild. I don't want to sound crazy or anything, but I was fascinated with rocks. There is a lot of Anasazi pottery in the area, and I would search for it. Whenever I would find something, I would take the pieces and try to put them together. Other times, I would just sit and listen to the trees and let nature in and that influenced my art style."

In other ways, Laura Lee and Jolene had similar childhoods. Jolene explains, "Like my mom, I did spend a lot of time with my grandmother when I was young. She, too, would tell us stories. Like my mom's grandmother, my grandmother had no electricity, no running water, and no bathroom, only an outhouse, but I would find a bush too! Also, I would herd sheep. I did have some of the same experiences as my mom."

Laura Lee thinks her own mom must be in her late eighties. "We are not really sure of the date of her birth. She was born in a hogan, and she does not have a birth certificate.

Laura Lee Yazzie

Maybe she was born in the fall when the crops were starting to be gathered. We kind of made up the date of September 24 for her birthday. She said that she was told it was when the leaves were turning brown, so we figured it was in autumn. We try to spend as much time with my mom as we can. She gets emotional when my kids are around. She gets really happy. They spent a lot of time with her when they were young. She kind of favors them."

Laura Lee continues, "My husband, Jackie, and I have five children and seven adopted children. Before we got married, when I was young, we knew of each other. Jackie was a jock in school. His mom was living close to my mom, and they were best friends. I could not afford clothes, and my mom did not speak any English, so she did not have any language skills. I would go over to Jackie's house, and his mom would measure me and make my clothes. I would see him around the house. He was always hanging out with his friends there, and he would ignore me. I was going to school in Holbrook, Arizona, at the time, and he was going to Valley High School in Sanders, Arizona. My grandmother, who was still alive, his mom, and my mom decided that we would have this arranged marriage. They made the decision when I was in the seventh grade. But the marriage took place when I was sixteen and Jackie was eighteen. It turned out OK.

"I tried to raise my children in a caring way. I wanted them to be good people. A lot of my teachings to Jolene were to help people, especially the elders and disabled. You are to greet the elders and say 'Hello' to them. That is what my grandmother taught me. Treat them like you want them to treat you. You are to be caring, giving, and just be honest. Your integrity and your character come from a long line of ancestors. My great-grandmother, my grandmother, my mom, they all passed it down. It is important to be a Native woman and to speak out on issues that you need to speak out on. Give your opinion, and don't let people tell you that your opinion doesn't count. As a Native woman you are not heard enough! Be a little bit aggressive, and if you have an opinion, speak it, especially if you stand up for something you believe in!"

Jolene holds up her skateboard painted with her artwork and says, "I had created a style before I went to art school. Once in school, I was able to develop it more. My theme became more of a woman warrior. The woman on this skateboard represents the women in my life, beginning with my mom. These women are solid, and sturdy, and are clear about what needs to be done. This painting represents the woman warrior. And this woman warrior is my mom."

> "My mom taught me to be a really loving person. She did not have to explain any of this. It was how she treated me."
>
> –Jolene (Bean) Yazzie

Laura Lee wants the best for her children. "I want them to have a good life. If my daughter had a job, then I wanted her to be happy in her career choice. Jackie and I encouraged them to go to school. They were not to come home and do nothing. We told them they needed to make something of themselves. All of our kids are pretty successful. They are living on their own now. They have their own families. I am really proud of my two daughters, and I am close to them. I think it is because they keep coming home for visits. They are always in contact with me. My boys are closer to their dad. But when they do call, they always ask for Mom."

Laura Lee strongly supports what Jolene wants to do with her life. Jolene declares, "I am not an artist to be famous. Some people want to be famous because they want to be out there, but I am holding back. I just want people to appreciate my art. I went to a technology school to learn about the computer, and I went to art school to create more of my artistic style, and the two fit together."

Laura Lee explains, "I want Jolene to contribute back to the community. She should share what she learns at school and share the talent she has. I think Jolene is on the right track."

Jolene N. (Bean) Yazzie

Jolene adds, "My mom taught me to be a really loving person. She did not have to explain any of this. It was how she treated me. She was a really good role model. My mom is strong and amazing. I think those two words capture her. She is very, very amazing."

Laura Lee says, "I get really emotional when I talk about both of my daughters. They are unique in their own ways. I am really proud of them. My one daughter went to Columbia University, and she is now a grandmother. Jolene wants to return to school to get her master's degree. We are very close, all three of us. We try to spend as much time together as possible. They are a joy to my life."

2021

Jolene Nenibah Yazzie shared that she prefers to be called "Bean," a nickname bestowed by her wife, Hannabah Blue. "I like it because it's gender nonconforming. We got married in 2019, five months before the pandemic hit the U.S. We currently live in Farmington, New Mexico, with our beautiful, sweet dog, Bella, and our two cats, Indie and Kiowa." The couple is starting a family.

Bean continued, "I am receiving my second bachelor's degree, in journalism, from Metropolitan State University of Denver this May. I am a freelance photographer, graphic designer, and artist. I recently did a piece for one of Joy Harjo's poems, and my art was printed in *The New Yorker* magazine for an art exhibition at apexart in New York, New York." Bean has presented her work in numerous shows, including a display at the National Museum of the American Indian in Washington, D.C. Her mother, Laura Lee, is her true inspiration and foundation of her work. Bean's art features strong Native American women as warriors.

Laura Lee's mother passed away five years ago. Laura Lee and Jackie still live in Lupton, Arizona. Fortunately, the entire Yazzie family is well. Laura Lee shared, "My husband and I are doing great. Our children and grandchildren are doing marvelous."

(Back, left to right) Daughter Jennifer Yazzie, Mother Carol Gonnie
(Front) Grandmother Helen Gonnie, Leupp, Arizona

Chapter 17

The Gonnie Family

"My mom was raised traditionally, but for me it was all about education."

—Carol Gonnie, June 17, 2012

Helen Gonnie's mother gave birth to her in a hogan in Gray Mesa at Donkey Springs, Arizona. Her aunties helped with her birth. Now age eighty-two, Helen shares how as a child she learned to weave a rug. Her daughter Carol translates for her. "I had to wake really early to herd sheep. Then I spent the rest of my morning carding and spinning wool. I always worked hard. My mother showed me how to weave with the wool I had spun. My mother was strict. There could be no fun, just herding and weaving from sunup to sundown."

Helen continues, "Life was hard in those days. We would cook with a fire on the ground. There were five brothers and two sisters. We cooked corn in many different ways. We had

Carol Gonnie and Jennifer Yazzie

no bread or flour. It was difficult back then. It was not like today when you can just open a can of corn or go to the store and get some chips. Also, we had to get our water. There was a spring where I was raised, and we had to haul water, so we had to walk a long way.

"Sometimes we would ride donkeys to get water and drive the wagon to get firewood. We made our own pots out of mud. My mother made the pots. I did not learn how to make them because I was herding the sheep. All seven children and two adults lived in the hogan. We slept on sheepskins; we had no blankets."

Helen did not have an arranged marriage; she wed at age twenty-three. She and her husband had twelve children. Luckily she had grandparents to help her with the child- rearing. Carol was close to her mother, and she grew into a tomboy to deal with her eight brothers. "My brothers were being mean to me, so I had to become strong." Helen liked the strength in her daughter.

Carol states, "My mom was raised traditionally, but for me, it was all about education. She had the herding and getting the rugs ready for weaving. She had a lot of work to do. I had a lot of work also, but it was with education. My mom stressed education for all of us. It was really important to her. She told us, 'Get an education, and when you are done, then you can get a job.'"

Carol continues, "I first went to preschool and then kindergarten. I attended boarding school at Leupp, Arizona, and in the eighth grade I went to school in Tuba City and lived in the Tuba City dorm. I would run away because I was having a hard time there. One time I made it all of the way home, and my dad took me back. During the 1970s we would go back and forth to the boarding schools in our wagon. I spoke Navajo for a long time, and it took me until the eighth grade to really learn English. Today I am a bus driver for Leupp Boarding School in Leupp. I drive 100 miles a day."

Carol enjoyed raising her daughter, Jennifer. Carol explains, "What I want for my daughter, Jennifer, is for her to go farther in education than I did. I wanted her to go to college. Jennifer did not go to boarding school when she was young. She went to preschool and then to Leupp Public School. She attended Tuba City boarding school when she was in high school. I feel like the boarding schools raised me, but I was able to raise Jennifer. In high school she was able to travel a lot because she was a good runner. She loved the boarding school because of the sports there. She even went to the Junior Olympics in track and field. She was supposed to get into the Olympics, but then she had her son. Today she still runs every morning." Jennifer works for the Navajo Nation Fire Department, and she is taking classes in fire science.

The loss of their home because of the Navajo-Hopi Land Dispute caused this family great sorrow. When they lost their land, they had to sell their livestock. Helen owned fifteen horses and 400 sheep. The Hopis bought her sheep for one dollar each, at an auction. Now Helen lives in a three-bedroom government house. Jennifer explains that her grandmother is sad she lost her land. But Jennifer and Carol are glad that she can take it easy because she is getting older.

Helen told Carol "to pray and offer prayers to the sun when it rises, sprinkling yellow and white corn. You are to bless yourself with cedar for safety before you leave anywhere on a long road trip. This is a blessing so you will make your destination."

Not only are they Grandmother, Mother, and Daughter, they are friends. Jennifer lives with her grandmother, Helen. Both Carol and Jennifer know that Helen goes "above and beyond. She breaks her back for anyone. If someone is in need, she says, 'Hold on! Let me finish this rug. I will sell it and give you some money!' Or, 'Let me make some blue corn buns to sell.' She is very traditional, and she wants us to pray every morning. I hear my grandma up in the morning, and I know that is my cue to get up and run. I run when the sun is about to rise. Grandma is a very traditional woman who is wonderful and happy. She is spunky and gets along with everybody."

Jennifer describes her mom, Carol, "as a strong lady who has been through a lot. She is a single mom. She is always on her feet and has been a busy woman trying to put food on the table for us." Jennifer in many ways follows in the footsteps of Helen and Carol. She, too, is a strong woman who gets along with people. All three want to keep their Navajo traditions alive.

Helen Gonnie

2021

Jennifer became a firefighter, but sadly, she passed away in 2016. Her mother, Carol, said Jennifer was a wonderful mother. Now Carol, retired as a bus driver, is raising Jennifer's son, Jayden. Carol states, "Grandson Jayden and I are doing well." Carol's mother, Helen, passed away in 2020 of kidney failure at the age of ninety.

Mother Marilyn Yazzie and Daughter Kaylene Yazzie, New Lands, Arizona

Chapter 18

The Yazzie Family

"Go to school and learn all you can. You can't get a job without a college degree. My daughter Kaylene has one degree in her pocket right now!"

—Marilyn Yazzie, June 6, 2011

Marilyn Yazzie's father had two wives; her father had nine children with his first wife, and then she died. "My father needed a second wife. In those days you could go and find a young girl and pay for her to be your wife. That was how we got my mother. She raised all nine of the first set of children and then had four more herself, one being me. We had a really large family. I was born in Nazlini, Arizona, in a hogan in the central part of the Navajo Reservation.

"When I was young, we had a framed house and hogan. In the summer, my mom would put us in the hogan. It was really crowded. My mom wanted us to learn to sleep on sheepskins. She would tell us to go and take the sheepskins outside in the morning and hang them on a log rack outside so they would air out. Then we would have breakfast, and it was usually corn meal mush. After breakfast, we would let the sheep wander out of the corral. We would hurry up and put on our jeans and tennis shoes and go after the sheep. They were all hungry, and we would take them to the watering hole. It was a little stream down in the canyon. We would follow them, and they would run to the water. On their way back, their bellies would be so full that they had to walk slower. That meant that we got to play. My cousins were all there because my mom and [her] sister got to live next door to each other. So the sheep were all combined.

"It would take a really long time for the sheep to come back and that gave us time to play paper dolls, not the punch-out kind you find in stores. We found the Sears catalog and would cut out and make our own. That is what we carried in a bag when we would herd the sheep. The boys would make cars out of boxes. We invented our own toys. They were not bought. We would play with these things while the sheep were returning to the corral. Once in the corral, we would have a snack before the big evening meal.

"We grew up in a house without running water. We had to go down to the canyon in our wagon. It was about three miles to get the water. We would put the water in a barrel. The horses would have to carry the water back to the house. We had to work really hard. We had to feed the horses and care for the sheep. There were cows around too.

"I did not want this kind of life for my children. My parents said that to us too. They also wanted it better for me than they had it. They would gather us together and talk to us about making our lives better.

"Now I have three children, two girls and a boy. I wanted all of my kids to have an education, which is what I told them when they were growing up. I said 'Always go to school no matter what. No matter how hard it is; you stay in school. That is what the world

Kaylene Yazzie and Marilyn Yazzie

expects out there. It is hard. You are going to grow up, and there are things you must know. So go to school and learn all you can. You can't get a job without a college degree.' My daughter Kaylene has one degree in her pocket right now!"

Marilyn continues, "I went to a boarding school when I was six. School was OK, but the dorm life was hard. It was a terrible experience for me. I went there speaking only Navajo and was forced to learn English. I was spanked for talking Navajo. One day my dad came there for a visit, and he saw bruises on my face. He asked me what happened, and I told him I got hit for speaking Navajo. So he took me out of school. But he did not put me back in another reservation school; he put me in a school off of the reservation in a town called Show Low, Arizona, with my sister and other white kids. He told me that I would learn English by going to school with white kids. I stayed there until I was twelve or thirteen years old. Guess what? I got so good in English that I didn't have to take it in Bible college. For high school I went to a parochial boarding school in Phoenix. That is where I picked up the faith and learned God's work.

"After high school I returned to the reservation and talked about my beliefs. I became a little missionary to my parents and especially my father. My father was a medicine man. He would do all sorts of different ceremonies for people in need. I would talk to him about being a medicine man. I would say, 'Dad, why are you doing this medicine man thing?' Then I say, 'Tell me, Dad, without reservation, don't hold back. What are you doing with these people? Do you think you are really making them well?'

"My dad would tell me, 'You talk to the people, and you find out what they are going through. Then you feed them back a diagnosis. Let's say a man was in the Army, and he was parachuting. I would tell him that he got thrown around in the air, and he needs a ceremony with another medicine man.'

"My husband and I talked to my dad about what our Christian God's word says. We talked and talked to him about the Christian God. The word says that our sins are forgiven and how we have a place in heaven. My dad finally said, 'OK I understand, and I know where you are coming from.' Soon he accepted Christ in his life. He did this long before he died. First he was a medicine man, and then he turned to Christ. In his old age he told me that I had to tell everybody about the message of Christ. I was to tell all of my siblings, my children, and my grandchildren. He wanted my husband and me to start a church at Nazlini. He even donated some land.

Kaylene Yazzie

"But about three months later, my husband came home and said that he had gotten the call to preach. He said that we needed to go to Nazarene Indian Bible College. We were going to move to Albuquerque, New Mexico. I told my husband that I did not want to go. 'We have a baby! How will we take care of the baby? How are we going to support this little child?' My husband said to me, 'God will provide. We are going to the Bible college so we can learn to help our people.' I grudgingly went because I wanted to give our children a better life than what we had. We concentrated on our studies until we got our degrees. In the summertime we would go out and help out at churches. That is how we found out about the relocation of homes.

"My husband lost his land in Coal Mine, Arizona, to the Hopis. They got control of that land called the Joint Use Area. All of the families living there had to scatter out. We were promised a new home. In 1989 we moved to New Lands near the Arizona and New

Marilyn Yazzie and Kaylene Yazzie

Mexico border. But trouble started before then. In 1974 the government told us to come Flagstaff to see if our name was on a list. This was a list to see if we had lost our land. Sure enough, there was my husband's name. We were living in Albuquerque at the time. The government said that if we were to come back to the reservation, they would build us a nice house. That is what they did. We got what we wanted in a house, but a lot of people did not get what they wanted because they did not speak English. They were not able to explain what they wanted.

"We started our church here in New Lands where we picked to live. We would have prayer meetings in the living room of our home. Now we have a real church. Hopefully as our children grow, they will see our lives and what we went through. I hope they will pick up our faith and still go with it. With the Navajo old ways there is no hope. When people were in trouble, they would pay another human being, a medicine man. That would not solve the problem because the problems are still there. When you serve God through prayer, then things happen. Our children get healed. You can see that God provides. I taught each one of my children to pray and serve the Lord.

"I tell them that their grandpa was a medicine man. I tell them what their grandpa said. He said, 'You know, I have lived a long time. I have tried all of the ceremonies you can think of. I have eaten peyote, smoked it, and chewed it, everywhere imaginable, but nothing helped me. And now you see me. I don't have any wealth. I just have my wisdom. I don't have a whole bunch of money that I can pass on to you because I have paid for all of these ceremonies over the years, and it has left me nothing. It left me a poor man. The only thing that spoke back to me was the God of the Bible. Read the written word. Learn all about it and tell others about it. This is what I say. God is the only one that spoke back to me.'"

When Kaylene, Marilyn's daughter, was young, her life was quite different from her mother's. Kaylene states, "I liked boarding school. I went to Sun Valley Indian School in

Holbrook, Arizona. My cousins were already going there. It was a parochial school, and my mom was able to visit. She could be there and visit whenever she wanted. She could be there on a daily basis. She was able to call me anytime. Also I would come home every weekend. That made a big difference.

"At the school, every morning we would get up between five and five-thirty. We would do our jobs and make our beds. Everybody had his or her own section to clean. On laundry day you had to take your sheets off of your bed. We had all of the chores before breakfast. When we got older, we would have a study hall in the morning. Then we had school. Next we had Bible classes and then sports, tutoring, or musical activities."

Kaylene explains, "During the summer when I was back at home, I would sleep in. I was supposed to care for my brother and my sister. We were to do chores like clean the kitchen and the living room. My parents were at work. We would watch TV and play. Then we would wait until the very last minute to start our chores. It was around three o'clock in the afternoon when we would begin."

The Yazzie family is close-knit, with the Christian God as their foundation. Marilyn had a traditional upbringing, while Kaylene's upbringing was quite modern. Both Marilyn and Kaylene have similar descriptions of each other. Marilyn states that Kaylene is loving, kind, and considerate, and Kaylene says that her mother has compassion and concern for her children and others. After these words, Mother and Daughter's eyes meet, fill with tears, and a tight hug follows.

2021

Kaylene, who married in 2014, had a baby girl she named Emily in 2019. Marilyn retired and is a "full-time grandma," caring for Emily while Kaylene works for the Sanders Unified School District. Emily is "two and a half and loves reading, playing outside, dancing, and

Marilyn Yazzie and Kaylene Yazzie

watching PBS children's programs. She is talking more and is picking up Navajo as well as English. My husband is retired . . . and we have our church to care for too.

"We are saddened to have lost precious loved ones to COVID during the past year. Our extended family was hit hard with COVID. Most have pulled through, but we have lost three brothers and a nephew. Then there are some who expired of natural causes. I have had my share of funerals."

(Back, left to right) Mother Farrah Lynn Begay, Grandmother Lucy Carlson Begay, Daughter Dayna Grey
(Front, left to right) Daughter Alicia Grey, Daughter Dariah Grey, Rock Point, Arizona

Chapter 19

The Begay Family

"We learned how to live from what my mom did and what my grandma did. It is what we still do. It is like a gift that keeps going on."

—Farrah Lynn Begay, June 10, 2011

Lucy Carlson Begay, age seventy-two, had four siblings; two brothers and two sisters. She and her siblings were born in the same hogan in her family's winter camp near Rough Rock, Arizona, and they used the resources of their land to live. Lucy, who speaks Navajo exclusively, had her daughter Farrah translate. "When I was young, we did not go to the store. Whatever we had to eat, we would grow right here. We would plant corn and live off of it and other things. We would drink goat milk and eat butchered goats and sheep."

Lucy raised her own children in this same area. Lucy and her husband have nine children; two boys and seven girls. Farrah, Lucy's youngest, says she was "babied" because she

Farrah Lynn Begay and Lucy Carlson Begay

was the last. Farrah, now age thirty-five, describes what life was like for her and her brothers and sisters. "There were more teachings back then. There was less technology, less television, more livestock, like sheep, goats, and horses. Children knew about responsibilities. They were raised with traditions and with teachings based on hard work and livestock. They had chores. When they were asked to do something, they would go and do it. The parents raised the young ones to be well disciplined. They really did not have any real difficulties growing up because all of the kids pitched in to do the work.

"They were different from how kids are nowadays. Today I see kids that talk back and do not work as hard. They are not taught how to live. They do not have respect and good family values. Our Native American skills are going away. Now life is different. I see a lot of the younger generation do not have a grip on the Navajo beliefs. We grew up as a traditional generation and to respect what is sacred. We strongly believe in our traditional values and our culture. The younger people belong to their parent's religion, but they do not practice it. They sit back and have their parents do everything for them.

"We learned how to live from what my mom did and from what my grandma did. It is what we still do. It is like a gift that keeps going on. In the winter days my grandmother would tell us winter stories around the fire. She would tell us stories about the emergence of the Navajo people. Sometimes she would sing when she was telling us a story. Hearing her stories was like watching TV. Today I wish I had notes of what she said to us. I wish I had a tape recorder of everything she said to us. To this day I only remember a little of it. That makes me sad."

Lucy regrets not having an education and not speaking English. Rosette, nicknamed Roz, another daughter of Lucy's and Farrah's older sister, translates for Lucy, saying, "When the school recruiters would come around, my parents would hide me and the other kids. But my sister got to go to school until the fifth grade. I could not go. I had to stay at home and do the weaving. The only money we had came from weaving. I did not go because I had responsibilities. My mother needed me to be with the sheep and the goats. Also, our horses would wander off, and I would always have to walk and find them.

"It was hard growing up in my day. We had no propane, and we had to gather wood for fires. We had to cook in the sunlight. There were no candles. We just went to bed when it got dark. We did learn a lot of life skills in order to survive. Those skills, our way of living, made us strong."

Even though Lucy was not able to be educated, she wanted schooling for her children, and that meant they would have to leave her every week. Roz attended Rough Rock Boarding School. She recalls, "We were lucky to come home on weekends. But when Sunday would come around, we would have to go back. A local person was to come around and transport us to school.

"Only this person did not want to drive all of the way out to our winter camp. My grandpa would put the three of us on his horse and walk us for miles. We would have our clothes and whatever else we brought home with us. We would meet the guy with the car with a bunch of kids in the back, and he would haul us to school. Grandpa would say goodbye to us, and he would say that he would see us next weekend, only Grandpa did not know what the word 'weekend' meant. Then he would give us each a quarter, which was a lot of money, to go shopping at school during the week. Seeing my grandpa leave, I would cry. From boarding school to our home would be a very long drive. I would cry and cry the whole way there.

"The school we went to was very special. Farrah and I went to a bilingual school. We had to learn our Navajo and English. We came to school only speaking Navajo and getting our English in gear was difficult. We would have math in English and then right after that, we would have math in Navajo, then science in English and science in Navajo."

Farrah adds, "Now that my husband and I are adults, we are both glad to be able to read and write in Navajo. We believe that learning both languages is sacred. So we teach our children, three daughters and another baby on the way. Sometimes our kids go crazy asking us questions. They say, 'What is this?' and 'What is that?' Sometimes they have tricky questions. We have to explain to them that sometimes there is not a name for something in Navajo. My oldest is able to understand Navajo, but for my youngest, it has been difficult."

Sister Roz continues, "We took on our mom's values and her language. We voluntarily learned the ceremonial teachings of things. We did it ourselves to carry on the traditions. My mother is proud that we carry them on. I had my *kinaaldá* ceremony at my mom's summer camp. I remember there were a lot of people. It was kind of embarrassing because the whole community knew that I was a woman. Actually it was good. The first person that I told was my aunt because my mom was not at home. My mom had so many girls that this was hard work for her. I remember my mom saying, 'Oh, dear.' But she was more than willing to have the ceremony for me. The ladies told me what to do throughout the ceremony. They chose my uncle to tie my hair and dress me up for it.

> "We took on our mom's values and her language."
>
> –Roz Begay

"When you have your womanhood, they choose somebody smart and a good worker. So they picked my uncle. He is a cook at Rough Rock School. After tying my hair, I started to run in the morning. My grandma was there, and my grandma taught me a lot. She taught me how to dress and how to become a woman.

"They put a lot of jewelry on me, and that was to represent how life was supposed to be. My mother's cousin brought me a heavy turquoise necklace. She put it around me during the ceremony, and I thought it was given to me. Then she says that it was not for me to keep, but it was to help me out. She told me that in the morning when I do things for my *kinaaldá*, this necklace will hold me down. She said that she was helping me because this will make me stronger. She explained that it would be heavy and give me more weight. It will make me tough, and I will be able to run and do women's work. This jewelry will help me in the future to push myself so I can do what I want to in life. The elders were also saying a lot of what was being said to me. So by the time of the final day, I had four concho belts and a whole bunch of necklaces and two or three bracelets on each side of me! It was really difficult for me because I had all of this stuff on me, and I could not run very well. But I was stronger for it. So I did what I was supposed to do during the ceremony, but it sure felt good when they removed all of the jewelry. I felt so light that I was ready to go into the world.

"When you have your *kinaaldá*, your hair comes down. You cannot brush away all of your problems by pushing your hair aside. You have to grind the corn and mix the corn. The ladies would bring their stirring sticks to the mixing of the corn. They would dig a hole in the ground and build a fire. By evening they put the corn mixture in the ground. They would cook it overnight. If you are very well disciplined, and if you are a nice girl, the cake will turn out good. Mine turned out good. The cake determines what kind of person you will be."

When school was out for the season, the Begay family spent time at their summer camp. Farrah remembers that her grandparents or parents would rouse her, her brothers, and her sisters at dawn. "They would wake us at four o'clock in the morning! We would have a breakfast of beans, cheese, goat milk, and our own homemade cappuccino, which was cooked cornmeal all nice and brown, put into coffee, which is also all nice and brown, plus sugar. Sometimes we would have tortillas warmed on the grill, which were really yesterday's fry bread. After our meal, we would herd the sheep out of the corral and

Alicia Grey

let them graze. While they were eating, we would do a lot of hiking and playing. Then, we would bring the sheep back in the evening.

"While the sheep were feeding, we had at times other jobs to tend to. We were told to get water over the hill. There were usually five or six of us there plus our cousins who lived close by, and they would be with us. We would take buckets, and we would get the water from the well. Next we would get a drink of water and wet our hair. We filled our buckets, and we started walking up the hill. We had to try so hard not to have the water spill out because we would want to bring back home as much water at one time as we could. We had a resting rock. We would hurry to the resting rock, so we could rest longer while the others were still suffering. Our water would last for about two days, and then we would have to do it again. We were told not to play with the water. We were told not to drink it all and not to waste it. If we wanted to wash our clothes or take a bath, we would have to go to the well. If the weather was dry and there was no rain, then there was no playing with the water. It was only for the sheep and for people to use for cooking and drinking."

Farrah talks about her grandmother and her own children. "As I told you, my grandmother would wake us up early. She told us that we were missing out on life by sleeping. She said that we had nothing to gain by sleeping. As much as I hated it, I, too, tried to get my kids up early. I don't believe in the media. I make them turn off the TV. I have them learn to do things. I have them align themselves with the modern culture and the traditional culture. This is something that is really difficult to do. My kids understand how to be respectful. They are to have respect for themselves and for everyone around them. My kids are kind, helpful, and do community service. I feel they appreciate themselves and others."

Roz says, "There is a whole world out there. You know, I took off from the rez. I lived in Michigan and then Texas. I moved to many different landscapes. I came back to the rez and then wanted to leave again. I fell in love with traveling. I wanted to join the Navy and cook in a culinary school, but my family and my culture pulled me back in. I did not belong out there. I wish I had started having kids earlier. I want to teach them the traditional values and the culture. I have already started. My kids are hard workers. We have horses, cows, lambs, goats, bunnies, chickens, and ponies. We have planted crops. The morning gods are all around us, and we greet them and pray to them."

Dariah Grey

Roz believes, "My parents did very well with all nine of us. All of us have our own horses. Most of us have our own sheep and goats. When it is time for planting or the irrigating or the building of fences, we all come back and help our parents. When it is time to cut the weeds or to harvest the corn, we come to help. We are a strong family with a great bond. We always help each other out. My brother, who lives in Tuba City, has his own cornfield, his own sheep, and horses. My sister is in Cow Springs, and she has her own sheep and cattle. I have my own little ranch, which is going really well. My other sister has many goats too. Most of my brothers and sisters continued in school. Some are educators and nurses, and they all have good jobs within their own areas. We are fortunate to have such strong and traditional parents. I think we all turned out to be OK."

Daughter Sarah Hendricks and Mother Sylvia Smith, Grey Mountain, Arizona

Chapter 20

The Smith Family

"When I was young, there was a goat that would always recognize me and then chase me. He knew who I was. . . . My mom would laugh and laugh when this would happen."

—Sarah Hendricks, May 1, 2010

Sarah Hendricks' parents raised her close to her grandmother's land in the Grey Mountain area, about thirty miles north of Flagstaff, Arizona. From her family's camp, a panorama of the San Francisco Peaks can be viewed. Sarah shares, "Our family always did a lot of moving around on our land to tend the sheep. We had to move where there was water. My mom did not encourage us to go for the sheep when we were young. But when we were older, she knew she could trust us to look after them."

Sarah spent her summers at her family's camp herding sheep; she was in school in the fall, winter, and spring. "I made the transition from school to home fairly easily. My mom always said that school was school, and sheep herding was sheep herding." At the age of five, Sarah attended Tuba City Boarding School, which is about thirty miles from her family's land. Her mom and dad would take Sarah and her six brothers and sisters in their wagon. "It was crowded with kids, and sometimes the wheels would come off. It was difficult to put them back on, but we would always do it.

"My first language was Navajo, and I had to learn English at the school." Her mom did not feel happy about that. "Even today as an adult, my mom says to speak only Navajo. She doesn't like us speaking English because she is not able to understand us."

Sarah describes her mom, Sylvia, as a hard worker. "At seventy-eight, she still weaves, herds sheep, and shears them. She even relocates the corral every time it gets too dirty. She never shovels the poop away. She just moves the corral from one place to another. She is very good at reusing things like mattress springs and parts of cars for the sides to her corral. My mom took one look at those old bedsprings, and she knew exactly how she was going to use them. She did the same with the hood of a car. All of this work she does by herself. My dad does not help. My mom makes little rooms in the corral for the lambs and their moms. This is so the lambs will know their moms, and the moms will know their lambs.

"When we were young, our sheep corral was our playground. We would make roads and bridges. We did not care that it was dirty. There we were, playing in the poop! We would play there for hours. Now I cannot stand the smell. When my mom comes to visit me in Flagstaff, I can smell it on her, and I don't like it.

"We only had sheepskin for our beds. We could not afford mattresses. We had to make sure that we put our heads the same direction as the sheep's head, not the sheep's tail. If we put our heads at the tail, then the sheep's wool might run off. That is what we thought. We all went to bed at the same time, including my mom and dad. It was crowded.

Sylvia Smith

"I was the one who would do a lot of the herding because I wanted to get away from the house. My sisters were always fighting. I couldn't stand the bickering. I would herd for many hours, and I would get thirsty. My grandmother thought it was weak to drink water while herding sheep. So when I was thirsty, I would drink from the sheep's trough! It was really muddy.

"We used to take the sheep up into the canyon. That is where we had our summer home. Taking them up the canyon was the hardest because the sheep were crying, but my mom was behind us, yelling to get them up. The sheep were pretty smart. They knew their master. They knew my mom's voice."

Sarah continues, "We have a scarecrow that scares the coyotes away. A few months ago a mountain lion showed up. We had puppies, and the mountain lion ate the puppies. Luckily the sheep were gone. My dad shot the mountain lion.

> "My grandmother thought it was weak to drink water while herding sheep."
>
> –Sarah Hendricks

"When I was young, there was a goat that would always recognize me and then chase me. He knew who I was. I would run away from him, and he would always run after me. I would run into the house all scared, and he would get on top of the house. My mom would laugh and laugh when this would happen.

"Sheep and goats are important to our family. We eat mutton and drink goat's milk. When there was a break in my dad's job, my mom would make rugs using the sheep's wool and take them to the Cameron Trading Post to sell. She would go by horseback. When she used the wide and thick yarn, it would take her about a week to make a rug. When she used thin yarn, it would take her a lot longer.

Sarah Hendricks and Sylvia Smith

"Now as an adult, I live in Flagstaff. I grew up without running water and electricity. Now I have plenty of both. I never try to change how my mom and dad live. I now live differently than they do. Seeing how my parents live was a total surprise to my husband, who is white. He had no idea at all. It took a while for me to get the courage to show him how we lived. I was wondering if he would stay with me after he saw how I grew up, but he was just amazed.

"We met in a grocery store in Flagstaff. I was a single mom. I was working in the store and was a student at Northern Arizona University. I would take classes, work at the store, and drive to my mom and dad's place every night. I had my kids with me. They would attend Flagstaff schools. I would do my homework under the kerosene lamp. In the morning there were showers at the trading post. I would take my kids there for showers, and we would start out the day driving back to Flagstaff. Their teachers had no idea how we were living. It took a lot for me to get my bachelor's degree. I am proud I have it. Now, I am a teacher in the public school system in Flagstaff.

"My mom is happy about my career. She is pleased with all of her kids' education because we did not come from much. She taught us physical health. We don't abuse alcohol or drugs. She would take us around to the alcoholics in town and tell us not to ever do that. She would tell us, 'Always keep busy. Get up early. There is no time for sleep. When you die, you will have plenty of time to sleep. When you are alive, you must be awake and busy.' That is my mom, always working, always active; she makes me proud."

Sarah Hendricks and Sylvia Smith

(Back, left to right) Mother Ophelia Goatson, Grandmother Vivian Descheny, Great-grandmother Rose Williams
(Front) Daughter Lela Goatson, Keams Canyon, Arizona

Chapter 21

The Williams Family

"I was born along the cornfields. . . . My mom did not know the month or the day. When the corn was two inches high, that was when I was born."

—Rose Williams, June 16, 2012

"I was born along the cornfields in White Cone, Arizona. I wasn't born in a hospital," explains Great-Grandmother Rose Williams. "My mom did not know the month or the day. When the corn was two inches high, that was when I was born. My parents decided it was May 5. They didn't know for sure. They just guessed it. My husband says that whenever the corn grows two inches, that is my birthday.

"When I was young, my mom got sick, and so I wanted to go live with my grandmother. She taught me a lot, like how to clean myself, and sew, and herd sheep. Early in the morning her sheep would be let out of the corral, and they would be on top of the hill. I would love to sit on the corral and smell the poop! I would be sitting on the fence and be waiting for the sheep to come back. When I was older and it was in the summer, I used to ride horses and herd sheep all day long. I would take them to the water and the windmill. I would love to sing, and I would sing for the sheep. Herding sheep, I would sing all day. The sheep would listen to me. My favorite memory is singing church songs, not traditional songs.

"My grandmother was a precious old lady. We lived in a hogan and a little house too. The soap we used was yucca. She would go and get the yucca from the ground, and she would wash my hair. She would brush my hair with a *bé 'ézhóó'* [grass brush]. I had a lot of hair. I had enough hair for two people. My grandmother would make it into a big bun of hair. She told me to never cut my hair. My hair represented rain. If you cut your hair, then you won't have any rain. When I got older, I cut my hair anyway. Also, my mom told me that along the way, I would get white hair, and she said to never dye it. If you dyed your hair, then God won't know you because your hair was not natural.

"My grandmother . . . told me to never cut my hair. My hair represented rain. If you cut your hair, then you won't have any rain."
–Rose Williams

"My grandma's favorite tea was Navajo tea. It smelled so nice and good. We would have that for breakfast along with pancakes and blue corn mush. She would drag me up early, and she would get the pan and milk the goat. With fresh goat milk, she would make the best pancakes ever. Sometimes she made the best fried chicken, and we would have that and blue corn mush for breakfast."

Education and being raised the correct way are important to this family. Rose explains, "During the school time I went to a boarding school in Lake Valley, New Mexico, and then when I was older, I went to a school in Crown Point, New Mexico, and then onto Gallup,

New Mexico. I graduated from Intermountain School in Brigham City, Utah. I worked in the Mormon Latter Day Saints bookstore for ten years in Salt Lake City, Utah. That is where I met my husband. The marriage was not arranged. We lived in Salt Lake for a few years. That is where I had my daughter, Vivian.

"We moved back to the reservation when Vivian was six. My mom kept calling for us to move back because she needed help with the herding and the shearing. So we moved back down here. I had to get used to it there on the reservation. At that time my mother did not have any running water or electricity. We had to haul water. Now we are lucky that we have both. We lost part of our land to the Hopis, but the government gave us this house that has water and electricity. It is much nicer and not so much work."

Daughter Vivian attended Toyei Boarding School in eastern Arizona and then a mission school in Holbrook, Arizona. "I cried when I went to the first boarding school," said Vivian. "When I went to my second school, the mission school, we weren't allowed to talk Navajo. If we did, then we would get our mouths washed out with soap. We would only eat vegetarian food. When we would come home, we would be desperate for mutton.

"My parents wanted to raise our family right. They wanted their children to respect people. So my brothers, and sisters, and I also went to the Seventh Day Adventist Church School. We were taught the Christian ways. They had a good attitude at that school."

Great-grandmother Rose did not have a *kinaaldá*. "I was in school when it happened. And my parents did not want to take me out of school. Both Vivian and her daughter Ophelia had one. Vivian wanted to continue the Navajo traditions."

When daughter Ophelia had her *kinaaldá*, she had to weave a rug in only four days. "I had to grind corn, and I had to behave and not cry. During this time I could not play with dolls. If I did, then I would have too many children. I had to have a good attitude. I had to run

Rose Williams and Vivian Descheny

and grind the corn like my mom. If someone told me to do something, then I would have to do it. I could not talk back!

"Besides passing down the *kinaaldás*, we also passed down the weaving. We are a family of weavers," explains Rose. "My grandmother used to weave in her hogan. She had four looms, and everybody would come and weave. My aunts and my grandma were all there. I was the only child in the hogan. My grandmother wanted me to sing while they were weaving. The only songs I knew were church songs. My favorite songs were 'This Little Light of Mine,' 'The B-I-B-L-E,' and 'Jesus Loves Me.' I would sing these songs over and over again. I finally would run out of singing, and then I would stop.

"I grew up with the weaving way," continues Rose. "My mom would weave, and I would spin the wool for her. My mom would use the natural wool to make a rug. My dad's mom was a great weaver. She taught me to weave, and I taught my daughters to weave. Vivian taught her daughter Ophelia to weave, and Vivian is teaching her son to weave."

Vivian talks about her weaving and says, "I was a divorced mom with three kids. I raised my kids by weaving. I put my kids through college with my weaving. My daughter Ophelia went to Northern Arizona University, and now she lives here in White Cone and works from home. She takes care of the needs of the at-risk families in the area. I wanted her to be a doctor, but she does not like the sight of blood. She wanted to help others who were in trouble mentally and emotionally. There is no blood in psychology."

Ophelia adds, "Weaving is what I grew up with. It was my younger brother, my sister, and me. My mom was a single parent. We were financially unstable. Weaving is what my mother did. She would use her money from the weaving to buy us food and school supplies. Weaving was good because she was with us all of the time. We would play around her. Weaving to me goes back to not just traditions, but it was a way of life for us. Sometimes she would be up all night and weave. We would ask her, 'When are you going to get done?' We were young and did not understand that a big rug would take her a really long time. Small rugs were quicker to finish. We were also so anxious when she had about two inches left. We would start getting ready for my mom to go and sell the rug. But then there was another challenge. Who would buy the rug? We would get our hopes up really high, and then maybe it would not sell.

"The three of us, my brother, my sister, and myself, know a lot about what my mom went through. Our dad never paid child support. Once there was a check in the mail, but it turned out to be only seven dollars. Now my mom has remarried and has two more children. My mom and stepdad both work. My mom works in a grocery store, and she weaves. My stepbrother and stepsister don't know about the life we had. They don't know how my mom came to be who she is now. When my mom was single and she had to weave, she would have a lot of orders so we would stay with my grandma and grandpa. We were fortunate to have our grandparents. They helped so much."

Vivian adds, "I was raised with a lot of love. My mom is my best friend. She has always been there for me. I am lucky to still have her. She has always been there for my kids. She has a very big heart."

Ophelia has the same feelings toward her mom. "My mom, I would say, is strong. She is the strongest lady I know. She has been my support system since I was small. If you had a problem or a worry, you would talk to her. She would help you the best way she could. I grew up without a father being there; she was my mom and my dad. When times got difficult, we were together. We made the best of it. She has a lot of heart. When she has something to do, then she puts her mind to it, and she always gets there. She doesn't see failure. The only way she knows is to continue to survive and thrive."

2021

Vivian said Rose, at "seventy-nine years, has been aging and has fallen many times. Sadly, she is no longer able to weave." Vivian's daughter Ophelia received her master's degree at Arizona State University and continues to practice social work in Flagstaff. A busy mother,

Rose Williams

she has four children. Her daughter Lela is now in the eighth grade and attends a charter school. Vivian's son Darvin, a rug weaver like his mother, attends the Institute of American Indian Arts in Santa Fe. Vivian started her own weaving business, called Southwest Weavers. She is known for her intricate designs and has won awards from the Santa Fe Indian Market, the Heard Museum, and the Museum of Northern Arizona.

Vivian's mom, Rose, shared, "Today I think back on what I did with my life and what I went through, and I am proud of my kids and grandkids. I am proud of being in the traditional way and sharing it with you."

(Back, left to right) Mother Tara Love, Grandmother Josephine C. Begay-James, (Front) Great-grandmother Desba H. Begay, Daughter Sheyenne Love, Flagstaff, Arizona

Chapter 22

The Begay Family

"I was to get up early, help with the sheep, cook and clean, wash clothes by hand, and make bread. I mothered the younger children, my brothers and sisters. Work was the norm."

—Josephine C. Begay-James, November 4, 2012

Desba H. Begay, born in a hogan near Coal Mine Mesa, Arizona, knows her birth date of November 24, 1934. Her daughter Josie shares about her grandmother giving birth to her mom. "In those days long ago, my grandmother gave birth using the old style, with a rope hanging from the logs surrounding the smoke hole of the hogan. Two women were there, and they acted like midwives to help my grandmother give birth. To the Navajo, the rope signifies the rays of the sun. My grandmother straddled the rope with a sheepskin below her on the ground. When my mom was born, the placenta was taken outside to a cedar tree and buried. [My mom's] umbilical cord was buried close by; this was so she would know where she came from. Inside of the hogan my mother's newborn head was placed toward the east for four days. My mom was fed corn pollen, which was known as the food of the sun. After four days my grandmother nursed her."

Josie adds, "Sadly, when my mom was young, her mother died. Then, raised by her grandfather's side of her family, she lived near The Gap area in Arizona. Even as early as age four, my mother would spend her days herding sheep and talking to them. For her it was difficult not having a mother. She felt as if she lived with the animals instead of her grandfather's family. She would even sleep with the sheep.

"As she grew older, she would rise around five o'clock, let the sheep out of the corral, and chase them into the fields. In the evenings she would card and spin the wool to weave rugs to support her grandparents. She was well versed in all aspects of the Navajo culture. She could ride horses, butcher sheep and goats, and keep the hogan clean. Her daily living was about survival. In the spring there was planting, hoeing, and weeding the twenty-acre field. In the summer there was always watering the plants. During fall there was harvesting and placing the vegetables in the underground cellar. Living was hard, and she was tired. Schooling was not part of her life."

Josie continues, "The teachings in the old days were that children were not to be weak. They were to be strong, and that is how she was viewed. It was more like the Depression era when children were expected to work. At times when my mom was herding sheep and was hungry, she would watch what plants the sheep would eat, and then she would eat those same plants.

"At the age of seventeen, my mother's life changed. One day she was coming back to the corral and noticed two women who were finely dressed coming to her grandparents' home. It turned out that these two ladies were coming to ask for her hand in marriage to one of their relatives. These ladies had seen her out and about and could tell that she was a hard worker. My grandparents said yes to the proposal, but they did not tell my mom until the day before the wedding!

"My grandmother began the conversation by telling my mom that they were going to dress her up the next day. She asked, 'Why?' When they told her that she was going to get married, my mother began to shiver like it was cold, and then she threw up. Physically shaken, she began thinking that she would run away. She kept crying over and over, 'Why are you doing this to me? Why are you doing this to me?' An old woman sensed she might try to take off and slept by her that night.

> "[My mom] could ride horses, butcher sheep and goats, and keep the hogan clean. Her daily living was about survival."
> –Josephine C. Begay-James

"The next morning my mom heard dogs barking. They were announcing the arrival of her soon-to-be husband and his family. There was a white tent near her hogan, and she ran into it and hid in a rolled-up sheepskin with blankets covering it. Everyone was looking for her. People were scouting around saying, 'Where did she go?' One of the menfolk who was standing close to the tent heard her because she threw up again. She was trying to hold it in, but she could not! He entered the tent, found her, and dragged her out and into the hogan.

"Inside, many ladies dressed her in beautiful clothes, and they gave her a blanket to cover herself. She wrapped herself up so tightly that she could hardly see out. Only her eyes were showing. Soon her uncle told her to follow him. She did not want to get married. It felt like she was being forced to get married, but she also knew she had to show reverence to her grandparents. When she saw this young gentleman, he seemed to be outgoing, laughing, and joking. She was even more frightened. She was shaking inside of the blanket throughout the ceremony. After the ceremony everyone started talking, and they were

(Back) Josephine C. Begay-James, Tara Love, (Front) Sheyenne Love

telling her how to be a good wife and a good cook. She just wanted them to shut up and not talk to her!

“Finally everyone left, and she was sitting by the fire with her new husband, my dad. She did not want to go to sleep. She did not know what to do. They both heard a dog barking, and they found her new husband’s saddle and some blankets all cut up. My dad told her that there might be people who did not want them to get married. People may have wanted him to marry another woman. These people were angry that my mother was chosen instead of another woman.

“My mother was not accustomed to a man. She did not want to be married. She did not like my dad, but she ended up having twelve children with him, and we all came out OK, so I guess everything was OK.”

Josie, born in Tuba City Hospital, also grew up in Coal Mine Mesa, Arizona. Her mom raised her with deep Navajo traditions of herding, shearing, weaving, and butchering. She sang Navajo songs and danced Navajo dances. Training horses and collecting plants became part of her activities. Her family lived off the land. No store was near. In the summer there was no water, and they had to haul it from the water tanks. The family would even wash themselves in the water the animals drank.

Desba felt glad her children attended school. Josie translated for her mom: “I did not have a choice for my kids. Going to school was the government law. The government came around and said this is the new law. Your kids have to go to school. Also I noticed that those people who were educated dressed really well, and they all had vehicles, and nice hats. I noticed that they had homes. I had nothing. I did not have an education. That is why I agreed to let my children go to school. I saw what I provided for my children was not enough. I saw my own kids struggling. At least at school they took showers and had electricity. I wanted my kids to have a better life and better opportunities. I wanted them to have it easier. I am happy that my children went to school, and that they have good jobs, and are not struggling.

"One other thing that I wanted for my children was to have them learn about the outside world. I listened to the teachers and others who believed that children who went off the reservation learned things from many people. So I had them go off of the reservation when they went to high school. They would have a new way of thinking. If they stayed on the reservation, everything is the same. I wanted my children to learn from other people. All of my children are very bright. They got scholarships. I did not have the money, but I wanted them to go and have a higher education. I never told them to study this or that. They chose what they wanted, and as adults they returned the favor and sent me money to help me out."

Josie adds, "I lived in two cultures. The boarding school was easy for me because I was already getting up early. I had to do things for myself like darn my socks. I was always independent, and I would help the less fortunate students and take care of them. Going to boarding school was where I learned about the dominant society. I learned a lot at the boarding school. I was in the gifted program and worked hard. When I got home, the expectations were still the same. I was to get up early, help with the sheep, cook and clean, wash clothes by hand, and make bread. I mothered the younger children, my brothers and sisters. Work was the norm.

"When time allowed, we would play outside. We would make animals out of sand and rocks. We would create rock carvings. We even played military and cracked open watermelons. After eating the insides, we would wear them as helmets. Then we would throw sand and rocks at each other. We had all homemade toys. Nothing was prefabricated."

Josie raised her own daughter, Tara, in Flagstaff, Arizona, where she attended public school. "Tara was like a tomboy growing up. She was known to go out and slug the boys. She was the cleanup girl when she was playing baseball. She was tall and slender, and the boys did not know she was a girl. She was an active child. Cheerleading, karate, volleyball, pageants, powwow dancing, and church were her interests. As a teenager, Tara was rebellious. I even planted a rose bush under her window so she would not sneak out."

Josie adds, "I was raised on the reservation, and Tara was raised off the reservation. My first husband was Irish, so I had to balance both cultures. But I wanted to keep Tara close to her Navajo culture. I used to take my children to the reservation during the summertime. I would take them out there to immerse them in their culture. One funny story is that Tara and her brother would pack a lunch and ride two billy goats while they were herding sheep. One goat's name was Kawa and the other's name was Saki. They pretended that these two goats were their motorcycles. They would call it 'wooly riding' and get bucked off. They had the greatest time herding sheep."

> "I would show my children videos and CDs so that they could learn about these traditional ceremonies."
>
> –Josephine C. Begay-James

Josie wanted Tara to know her Navajo culture well. "I made sure that Tara would always help with traditional ceremonies like the Enemy Way, where there is the undoing of harmful happenings to a person. And in the summer Tara would help with the squaw dances, where young women would invite young men to dance. I would show my children videos and CDs so that they could learn about these traditional ceremonies.

"I know in the outside world, in the dominant American society, that attorneys and doctors do very well. Physician assistants do well too. I have researched these positions. I did not wait to educate myself. I sought knowledge. So I told my children to do something that gives you money so you can buy a home, so you can stand on your own two feet and make money. Be the best at what you can be. If you chose to be a ditchdigger, then be the best ditchdigger you can be. I don't care what occupation you choose, just be the best at that. I have left it up to my children, just like my mother did with me.

"I went to college when I was sixteen. I graduated when I was twenty. My undergraduate education was in special education and elementary education. At age twenty-one, I was a guidance counselor for the school district in Flagstaff, and I also bought my own home. I was able to teach all kinds of classes such as special education, elementary education, Diné studies, and Diné language. I am a motivational speaker, a cultural specialist, and I have given workshops and presentations to educators. I retired at age fifty-four and am now a guidance counselor at Greyhills Academy High School in Tuba City, Arizona. I have been in the education field my whole career. I want my children to find a career that they are satisfied to have."

Daughter Tara has a degree in hospitality and was in the Army for eight years. She was the first female to return to Flagstaff from Iraq. Now she is a financial aid advisor for a local college. Tara adds, "My mom expected us to be independent. She told us not to be dependent on her. She would be there to support us like a backup. She taught me that I needed to learn to live on my own. I might trip and fall, but I know I am to get up again. This is what my mother taught me, and I am teaching the same to my daughter, Sheyenne, age ten."

Sheyenne, described by her mom as a worldly young lady, traveled and lived in many places throughout the United States. Because of her travels, her mom labels her as an Army brat. Tara talks about Sheyenne. "When I ask her what she wants to be, she tells me that she wants to help people and animals. She is interested in environmentalism and in taking care of Mother Earth. I tell Sheyenne, 'OK then, you have to do your best in school and be the master of your own destiny. You must make sure that you are well versed and knowledgeable because you can only rely on yourself. Even if you stumble, you can't expect someone else to pick you up. You will need to do this yourself. You should know to do your best, so you can have doors opening for you as opposed to doors closing.'

Sheyenne Love, Tara Love, Josephine Begay-James

"Sheyenne has said that she may want to be an astronaut or a pilot, so we took her to Lowell Observatory in Flagstaff. She would like to be the first Navajo female in outer space. When she was seven, she asked if she could drive. I told her that if she could reach the pedals, which she could, then she could start driving. At the age of eight she knew she needed to be able to shoot a gun. So we taught her how to shoot. Still later she wanted to be able to protect herself, so she took Tae Kwon Do. Sheyenne tells me what she needs at the time. My job is to equip her to be the wonderful person she is meant to be and not tell her who she is."

> "My mom knows that life is a fight, and you have to be equipped."
>
> –Tara Love

Tara describes her daughter Sheyenne as a little mother. "Her friends call her 'Mom' like my friends call me 'Mom.' Sheyenne is always willing to help, and she is a very determined young lady. When she sets her mind to do something, she gets it done! Wanting to make the world a better place, she does fundraising for those in need. I see in the Navajo way a lot of people baby their children. In our family we do not think children are babies. They are small adults. When they are young, we help them to live and require certain things from them. Her friends say I am strict. I talk to her as a small adult because she is responsible for herself. I tell her, 'What if I am not here. What are you going to do?'"

The teachings that Tara gives to Sheyenne came from Josie and in turn, Desba. The traditions and values have been passed down from one generation to the next. Josie describes Tara as a hard worker, dedicated to helping people. She understands the needs of all kinds of people.

Tara labels Josie similarly. "She, too, is a rock for many people in the community. Strong and motivating, people come to her for advice and spiritual direction. She is a good role model for the community. My mom knows that life is a fight, and you have to be equipped. My mother was strict, but I see her more caring part with my own children and external people."

Like her daughter, granddaughter, and great-granddaughter, Desba is hardworking and kind. A strong woman physically, she builds hogans, hauls water, herds sheep, and then cooks at night. She possesses clarity in giving guidance and direction to her family. Knowledgeable about the Navajo ways, she understands the importance of what Navajo gifts to pass to her children and their children.

2021

Josie explained, "My mom is in a nursing home in Flagstaff, and she's eighty-nine years old. She had a spine injury, and that's why she's in a wheelchair." Her children tend to her camp near Tuba City and her garden in Curley Valley, Arizona. Because of COVID, Josie mentors, tutors, and supports her granddaughter during virtual school. Her son had a traditional Navajo wedding in Grey Mountain and now has a baby son. The family just had the baby's first laugh celebration.

Josie's husband, a medicine man, offers ceremonies. "We know it's important to stay safe. Those who need a blessing send their photos, and my husband asks their needs and offers prayers. He talks with them on the phone. It's important to keep the traditions alive and going even though we cannot be together. I have a three-acre ranch with sheep, horses, and a hogan in my backyard. We just butchered a sheep for friends coming for a visit."

Daughter Tara is the business manager for the City of Flagstaff. Granddaughter Sheyenne graduated from Flagstaff High School taking AP classes and was accepted to Northern Arizona University, entering the College of Engineering. Her freshman year had to be online, and she also works at a local restaurant. "She is a busy girl," Josie said.

Navajo Hogan, Kayenta, Arizona. Navajos past and present use hogans for shelters and ceremonies, constructing them with logs, rocks, and mud.

Chapter 23

The Impacts of History

The Long Walk

The Southwest became part of U.S. territory with the signing of the Treaty of Guadalupe Hidalgo in 1848, at the conclusion of the Mexican-American War.[19] This vast territory included California, Nevada, Arizona, New Mexico, Colorado, and Texas.

Conflicts soon arose. Military leaders took notice of the strength, power, and wealth of the Navajo. The first U.S. governor of the New Mexico Territory informed the federal government that the Navajos "possessed 30,000 cattle, 500,000 sheep and 10,000 horses along with expanding fields and the ability to create long-lasting blankets with exquisite designs."[20] Fearing they would become too powerful, the U.S. military was afraid of Diné wealth and supremacy. The influx of American settlers traveling west through Navajo territory raised concerns for the pioneers' safety. The concept of Manifest Destiny, used by Anglos to justify taking land, created a sense of entitlement.

Treaties drawn up with the U.S. government turned out to be inconsistently honored, partly because Navajos did not have a single leader with whom to negotiate. One Diné group would sign a treaty while others would not be informed, thus earning the Navajo a reputation of untrustworthiness.[21] Yet Navajo resistance continued even as the government established military strongholds to protect American settlers. Angered and frustrated, Congress and the Army turned to more brutal practices.[22]

Military officers planned to kidnap as many Diné as possible from their land and march them to a new location, a great distance from *Dinétah* (The People's homeland). American settlers believed this would allow them to live on Navajo land, develop it for farming, and use its other natural resources.[23] Some predicted gold could be found there. Earlier successes in forcing other Southeastern tribes to reservations made the military certain the same would occur with the Diné. Furthermore, the American government believed the time had come for The People to be "civilized." They would be "tamed," disciplined, and pressured to adopt the white man's ways by moving them off of their Navajo land.[24]

In eastern New Mexico, the military selected Fort Sumner for the Diné, a desolate site not conducive to habitation. Its water source from the Pecos River carried bitter-tasting alkali compounds, which made it unhealthy to drink. Bringing in building materials and food supplies turned into a lengthy process because of harsh geography and weather conditions.[25]

The Army needed an experienced leader to move The People to Fort Sumner (also called *Hwéeldi* or the Bosque Redondo Indian Reservation), and it selected frontiersman Kit Carson.[26] Carson gathered Ute and Hopi men eager to join him in combat after warring with the Diné for years.

Carson and his soldiers attacked Navajo camps, burned hogans and orchards, shot resisters, killed sheep and other livestock, grabbed remaining Diné, and forced them to trudge hundreds of miles.[27] Not being a unified tribe, the Diné were spread over their vast region to allow for plenty of grazing for their sheep. Driven to kill or capture every Navajo, Kit Carson and his troops carried out horrific assaults on Navajo country to imprison The

People.[28] The captives did not know where they were going or why. Many were exhausted and malnourished when they started, and more than 200 died along the way.

Hwéeldi, Fort Sumner

Once the military processed the Diné at Fort Canby, the soldiers marched them more than 200 miles to Fort Sumner. "It was not a single event . . . but fifty-three different episodes of the Long Walk, dating from August 1863 through the end of 1866."[29] Moccasins tore and offered little protection. Extreme summer temperatures stifled the Navajos, and bitterly cold winter months brought ice and snow. Starving and wearing rags, The People plodded along day after day. Pregnant women gave birth while traveling on route; one was shot because she might slow down the trek, and others were killed for being sickly. Many struggled to stay upright, while others died.[30] Author Peter Iverson states, "The Long Walk was not a walk. It was a force-march driven by harshness and cruelty."[31]

Once at Fort Sumner, the Diné encountered desolate, rugged, and treeless lands. Those who arrived first constructed the fort and their detention center. During construction, Navajos survived without much shelter and clothing. The People dug pits, covered the holes with pine boughs or blankets, and called them home. Feeding the Navajos proved difficult for the Army. Attempts to grow crops failed. Several years in a row, the Diné cleared land using their bare hands and sticks, only to have cutworms destroy the plants. Finally the military issued rations. The food, foreign to the Navajo diet, arrived spoiled, and without enough to eat, many starved to death.[32] The government had expected to keep about 3,000 Diné prisoners, but eventually 8,000 arrived. With overcrowded conditions, The People lived with filth and disease, "barefoot, dressed in rags, suffering from exposure, and dysentery."[33] Firewood, being difficult to locate, made the brutal winters miserable. Yet in spite of the physical and emotional pain, The People continued to survive.

Lucy Carlson Begay's Sheep and Goat Corral, Close to Rock Point, Arizona

By 1867, the military's challenge to isolate and "tame" the Diné had been labeled a complete failure. The government realized the time had come for the Navajos to leave Fort Sumner. The People signed the Treaty of Bosque Redondo, also known as the *Naal Tsoos Sání* (Treaty of Fort Sumner) on June 1, 1868, agreeing to several conditions, including stopping all wars with the U.S. government, living only on designated lands, and allowing railroads through their territory. In July, 7,000 Navajos started toward their homeland, some riding in wagons and others walking in a procession stretching ten miles. Escorted by cavalry soldiers, many Diné wept with joy when they first saw their sacred mountains close to their *Dinétah*. After four years of anguish and extreme poverty, The People had finally returned to their homeland.[34]

One consequence of The Long Walk and the imprisonment at Fort Sumner was a unification of The People. Before Carson's raiding, many different bands of Diné had settled over a vast territory for better grazing opportunities. Imprisoning them at Fort Sumner brought about a unification, as they became one people.[35]

Even though the Diné survived brutal conditions, they did adopt various ways of living from their captors. Navajo women used new types of yarn for weaving blankets. Men learned irrigation farming and silversmithing. Flour, once a foreign food ration, now was used to create fry bread, a staple at Navajo meals. Coffee, also new to Navajos, turned out to be a popular beverage. Men discarded animal skins and changed to cotton pants. Diné women adopted the long skirts and loose blouses worn by Fort Sumner military wives.[36] Today, many traditional Navajo females wear this style while living their daily lives. They herd sheep, chop wood, weave rugs, shop at grocery stores, and eat at restaurants while wearing the same outfits as the soldiers' wives of the 1860s.

The internment at Fort Sumner was a dark period for The People. Even though the Diné suffered horrific atrocities, their inner strength and desire for their children's future pushed them to stay alive. Most of the participants in this book had ancestors who survived The Long Walk. Three families (Bertha Fuson and Jennie Haag, Kim and Lena Yazzie, and Marie Nez and Mable Wauneka Goodwin) spoke of the land that was given and the family relationships that resulted from the four years of suffering. All present-day Diné know of this tragedy; it has not been forgotten.

The return to *Dinétah* ushered in a period of peace and prosperity, but that later changed. Those who had survived The Long Walk faced a century-long dispute that would result in misery and devastation for both Navajos and Hopis.

Navajo-Hopi Land Dispute

In 1868, when the U.S. government released the Diné from Fort Sumner, they returned to their lands, relieved to be settled. The government had allotted each Navajo family at least one male and one female sheep. Eager to prosper again, the Diné soon expanded their small herds into larger ones.

They did not know that in the near future, the U.S. government would allocate some of these lands to the Hopi. The government failed to erect fences or post signs designating boundaries.[37] Navajo and Hopi families lived side by side on Hopi-allocated land, intermarrying, gathering for festivals, trading with each other, and helping one another, although some Hopis pointed out that according to the federal government, the land was theirs.

The Executive Order of 1882 issued by President Chester Allen Arthur complicated the situation. It affirmed "the use and occupancy of the Moqui (Hopi) and such other Indians as the Secretary of State might see fit to settle thereon."[38] The phrase "such other Indians" proved to be problematic. At the time, federal government officials viewed all Indians as one people, not recognizing that hundreds of tribes existed or that Hopi and Navajo families intermarried.[39]

> This act and the resulting relocations caused enormous distress and cultural upheaval.

Navajos concluded they were the "such other Indians" in Arthur's order. To make matters worse, Washington officials did not communicate the Order of 1882 to all Diné. Once again, the government failed to designate Hopi boundaries, and borders were not identified. Navajos continued to expand their herds in the Hopi-allocated area.[40] According to Peter Iverson, author of *Diné: A History of the Navajos*, "The 1882 Order practically ensured conflict between the two peoples, since it failed to clarify which land should be occupied by the Hopis or the 'other Indians.'"[41]

Six years after the Executive Order, the U.S. Secretary of War sent troops to the region to order Navajos to remain in "their own territory." The soldiers were advised not to anger the Navajo because Fort Sumner remained in their minds. However, "The troops noted that no boundary markers existed. It was easy to see how Navajo sheepherders could stray onto the government-allocated Hopi lands."[42]

Some Hopis continued to object, but the federal government did not listen. These objections led to much debate about who had rights to the land. Many Navajos knew they had occupied this region long before Fort Sumner. Navajo families continued for decades to survive with their hogans, corrals, and sheep on a portion of the Hopi Reservation.

Not until the 1930s, when the energy industry became interested in coal, oil, and uranium on this disputed land, did the federal government begin to take note. In *The Wind Won't Know Me*, author Emily Benedek elaborates, "It was not repeated Hopi complaints . . . that drove the government to action. It was the pressure of oil and gas companies to determine ownership of the area." Benedek quotes Hopi traditionalist Thomas Banyacya, who said, "The land will fall to mineral development. If this happens, we will find ourselves with our bedrooms on our backs. The law is doing this to all native peoples."[43]

Many court cases ensued. Attorneys for both tribes pushed for ownership of the disputed area. In all, the disagreement resulted in twelve state court cases, eighteen federal lawsuits, and three federal statutes involving over 1.8 million acres of land. In December 1974, Congress passed the Navajo-Hopi Indian Land Settlement Act. In 1975, Judge James Walsh from the District Court of Arizona drew a line down the middle of the land—one side to be owned by Hopis and the other by Navajos.[44] Over 100 Hopi and 10,000 Navajo people had to move; of the latter, many were of Navajo and Hopi ancestry.[45] These shared lands were then designated as the Joint Use Area.

This act and the resulting relocations caused enormous distress and cultural upheaval. For both tribes, land holds identity and is a source of self-understanding, history, and religion. For the Navajo, "Hogans are built on it. Ancestors' bones lie in it. Umbilical cords have been buried in their animal corrals or beneath the women's looms. These acts are to ensure a connection to the camp and the earth. Asking the Navajos to leave meant asking them to abandon the repository of their memories, the land which they have learned to master, the sites through which they communicate with their gods."[46] The Hopi "grazed cattle on it, planted cornfields on it, gathered wood from it and traveled over it to visit shrines and collect eaglets."[47]

Congress's vote to approve relocation created a nightmare for those who had to move. Many of the relocated Navajo suffered from severe depression, as the land was so deeply woven into every part of their essence. They could no longer tend their sheep and grow crops. It broke their hearts to be disconnected from their land.

For Navajo Stella Worker, who lived close to Leupp, Arizona, the thought of losing her land made her heart ache. Her children's umbilical cords, buried near her corral, bound her youngsters to the land and sheep. She prayed she and her husband would be able to stay where they had raised their family. Unfortunately, this did not happen. Through the kindness of a relative who gave them a small parcel on the reservation, the couple relocated about ten miles from their home, where they lived in a three-bedroom prefab house with no water or electricity.

The Diné who relocated to border towns experienced the trauma of leaving traditional ways. The federal government issued money to each family, but it was barely enough to purchase a house and have anything left to sustain family members. The skills learned on the reservation did not translate into the white man's world of work. Herding sheep, making yucca shampoo, or building a hogan were not skills that provided work in Anglo towns and cities. Many who did relocate to border towns returned to the reservation, usually to live with relatives.[48]

Many of those who relocated did not buy into the concept of ownership of land because spiritually, the land is their Mother Earth. Josie C. Begay-James asks the question, "How can you own your mother?" To the Diné, the land belongs to everyone, and Josie answered her own question, "Nobody can own land."

Helen Gonnie related the pain and confusion when she left her land. She shared, "It was really hard to move. It broke my heart. I keep asking why I had to leave my land. Now I live in a house. I live in a neighborhood with many houses. There is nothing to do here. When I lived on the land, I had animals. Now I have a house, not a hogan. I had to sell my animals. I have no sheep. I have no horses. I lost how to live."

The families of Rebecca Zee, Lena Yazzie, Rose William, Marilyn Yazzie, and Helen Gonnie relocated as a result of the dispute. The families of Lena Yazzie, Rose Williams, and Marilyn Yazzie spoke English and were able to tell the federal government the kind of homes they wanted. Sadly, those who spoke Navajo exclusively and were unable to express their needs, such as the families of Rebecca Zee and Helen Gonnie, received a cement-block three-bedroom, one-bathroom house on a small plot of land. Witnessing their sorrow still remains difficult.

Boarding Schools and Education

Another result stemming from the Treaty of Fort Sumner was the stipulation that Diné children be educated in the ways of the white man. The treaty called for the federal government to provide a teacher and classroom for every thirty children who could be "induced or compelled to enroll."[49] To this day it is not certain that Navajo leaders understood the terms of this agreement and its implications for their children and families.

The Presbyterian Church sponsored the building of the first one-room adobe schoolhouse in Fort Defiance, Arizona, in October 1869. At once, the school faced problems, not the least of which was low enrollment and attendance. Diné children, busy with family and camp chores, had no time for government education. They would attend two or three days, then not show for another four. Distance also made attendance difficult.

Navajo families followed their sheep to different locations in summer, winter, spring, and fall so their animals would have fresh grass. Not long after the new school at Fort Defiance began, it failed.[50]

Navajos were leery of white men's schooling. The Diné already had a system of education where mostly women educated the children in "the preservation of the language, ceremonial knowledge, social organization, weaving, and former subsistence patterns."[51] Diné children learned to haul water, chop firewood, plant crops, and tend livestock. Their curriculum centered on living in balance and harmony with the land and in ceremonies connected to the earth.

Not to be dissuaded, government Indian agents were certain that boarding schools would be a far better solution for re-educating Diné children. This concept would eliminate the problem of attendance and provide an easier way to end the teachings of Navajo traditions and religion. The government determined that the more distance between tribal lands and Native children, the better. Boarding schools were established as far away as California, Utah, and Pennsylvania. "The primary objective of Navajo schools, those operated both by Christian missionaries and the Indian Bureau, was to eradicate Navajo culture."[52]

> Government agents kidnapped Diné children ages six to sixteen from fields at gunpoint and forced them into schools.

By the 1880s, Navajos and other tribes were resisting the boarding-school movement. Undeterred, government agents kidnapped Diné children ages six to sixteen from fields at gunpoint and forced them into schools. Some would not see their families again for four or five years. During that same decade Congress passed the Compulsory Indian Education Law, which required parents to send their sons and daughters to boarding schools. To save money, ". . . boarding schools were turned over to mission groups from the Presbyterian, Methodist, Catholic, and Christian Reformed churches, among others, as Congress believed that Christianization and acculturation of the Indian could be encouraged with little expenditure from the government."[53]

Life at boarding schools turned out to be a catastrophe for Native children. Students marched to and from class. They could not speak Navajo, even to fellow students. Teachers gave instruction in English, even though boys and girls came to school speaking Navajo exclusively. Students caught speaking their primary language were punished severely by handcuffing their wrists and ankles, and washing their mouths with lye soap. Poor nutrition, unclean conditions, and overcrowding led to frequent outbreaks of disease. Students were not allowed to wear traditional dress and hairstyles. The children suffered homesickness, and some ran away. When they were captured, employees locked the children in closets as punishment, with food denied for several days. Boarding school education included church attendance and attempts to convert students to Christianity. Missionaries running the schools sought to eliminate the Diné religion, forbidding Navajo singing, chanting, or references to ceremonies.[54]

Diné daughters and sons who finally returned to their Navajo homes after completing a boarding school education felt confused and conflicted. Boarding school personnel expected Native students to persuade their families to follow Anglo ways. Instead, children faced strong resistance from their parents. Families realized that a boarding school education was a brutal attempt to abolish the Diné culture. Their children's treatment caused alarm. Finally, parents demanded day schools and boarding schools be built on reservation land.[55]

By 1933, the government's approach to Native education had changed radically. The Bureau of Indian Affairs recognized the need to educate Diné children within their own society. The federal government finally constructed more and more day schools and boarding schools on reservations.[56]

Navajo Jennie Haag remembered a time during the mid-1950s. "When I was six, I had to go to a boarding school. A Bureau of Indian Affairs man came and took me in the fall season. I only saw my parents at Christmas and the summer. At school we had to keep everything clean. An instructor would come by and check. We had to learn to speak English and how to read and write it." Besides teaching reading, writing, and math, teachers added Navajo history to the curriculum. From 1951 through 1958, the federal government funded $32 million for new schools.[57]

To complete the story of white-controlled Navajo education in the Southwest requires mention of the Indian Student Placement Program run by the Mormon Church from 1954 through 1996. The church placed Diné students in Mormon homes, often at the request of Navajo families who felt their children would be better cared for and educated than in their own homes. Mormons felt called to this effort, believing they fulfilled a Mormon prophecy. To them, Native Americans were the "chosen" people and the descendants of the ancient House of Israel. Mormons believed it was their calling to convert the children they took in. After forty years, the program ended when the last student graduated in 2000.[58] Rose Williams; Jean, Lisa, Mindy and Lolita Mann; Edith Puente; and Kathy Powell left the reservation during their childhood years to live with Mormon families or in similar programs.

Many women interviewed for this book expressed bitterness about their boarding school experience. They encountered great distress by the cruel treatment and had difficulty sharing what happened to them. Others felt differently, indicating approval of their schooling because they were fed adequately and kept warm. Most elders said that they did not attend school because their parents needed them to tend the sheep and weave rugs.

Each Navajo generation in *Voices of Navajo Mothers and Daughters: Portraits of Beauty* wanted the next generation to live a life better than theirs. Mothers stressed not wanting their children to grow up the way they did. They did not want to see their children living in poverty, without running water and electricity; they longed for a comfortable standard of living for them. To these mothers, education was the answer. But for Navajo families, where and how to pursue that education has always been a difficult choice.

In the Introduction, I questioned if changes had occurred since I lived at Dilcon Boarding School more than thirty-five years ago. From my interviews, I sensed the culture was still strong, especially within elders and "Navajo baby boomers." The millennials, fearful that Diné traditions could be lost with the passing of both generations, were driven to keep their heritage alive. These young adults understood that being educated gives them the power to preserve their culture in new ways. Stories and traditions have been documented and practiced. Today, teachers instruct students in Diné history, culture, and language in northern Arizona schools.

I found it interesting to learn the educational levels held by each generation. Only two out of the eleven elders in the book had some form of instruction. Yet, they strongly emphasized its need, and most felt deep regret about not being educated. All of the Navajo baby boomers interviewed for this book obtained a high school education except for one, and she attended school through the sixth grade. Some had schooling after high school. The outcome of these mothers' emphasis on education proved successful. Every millennial in *Voices of Navajo Mothers and Daughters: Portraits of Beauty* graduated from high school and continued with college or vocational school.

The Global Pandemic

In early 2020, the Navajo Nation was struck hard by COVID-19. Navajo Nation President Jonathan Nez called it an invisible monster. "When the virus came here to the reservation, it took off like wildfire."[59] The virus spread swiftly in part because many Navajos live in multigenerational homes. In addition, about one-third of the population of more than 300,000 do not have a tap or flushing toilet.[60] By May 2020, the reservation's per capita infection rate was the highest in the country.

President Nez took decisive action, requiring masks, closing roads and businesses, asking residents to shelter-in-place, and enforcing strict weekend curfews. Soon, infection and death rates plummeted, and a year later the Navajo Nation was a model of success for the rest of the country. President Nez stressed that "it was not about the loss of personal freedom but caring for each other, the philosophy of the greater good."[61]

Since the arrival of the vaccine, Dr. Loretta Christensen, Chief Medical Officer of the Navajo Area Indian Health Service, has noted, "The success comes in administering the vaccine due to planning and high-level cooperation."[62] The Navajo Nation, the Indian Health Service, and tribal health officials jointly achieved a successful vaccination rollout. By March 2021, the Navajo Nation had vaccinated more of its population than any state and led the nation in vaccine implementation.

Navajo Hogan Woven Ceiling, Kayenta, Arizona

Afterword

The Heart of Family and Culture

My original wish in *Voices of Navajo Mothers and Daughters: Portraits of Beauty* was to satisfy my curiosity in how Navajo women live today as compared to thirty-five years ago when I lived on the reservation. In hindsight, I recognize my thinking runs deeper than simple inquisitiveness.

Whether it is 1977 or today, I marvel at these women. I am grateful they invited me into their homes and opened up their lives. At times, I sensed my questions might be too personal, but they still responded, sometimes with deep emotion. To me, their stories are fascinating and at times shocking. They face such a difficult physical and emotional lifestyle: hauling water, chopping firewood, caring for grandmother, planting crops, raising children, tending livestock, keeping their culture preserved, maybe working full-time.

Many Diné mothers and daughters thanked us for the opportunity to share the stories of their lives. Some learned new information about their families, and others acquired details they had always wondered about, but been afraid to ask. The women enjoyed sharing humorous experiences or were saddened by talking about tragedy in their lives. In every interview, laughter and tears occurred. A few weeks after an interview, I met with one of the daughters. She described our meeting as touching and meaningful for her and her mother.

Throughout our conversations, I experienced Navajo women of all ages as the heart of family and culture, combining new ways of modern society with old traditions. Now, I understand that this project is about more than satisfying my curiosity; it's about honoring these amazing women because of who they are and what they have accomplished.

Laura Lee Yazzie's Journals, Lupton, Arizona

Scene Near Leupp, Arizona, With the San Francisco Peaks

Acknowledgments

To begin, I offer a heartfelt thank you to the twenty-one Navajo families who participated in *Voices of Navajo Mothers and Daughters: Portraits of Beauty*. Sharing personal experiences of their lives took courage. These mothers and daughters are the essence of this work. I appreciate the time they spent with me and the opportunity to learn about their lives and hear their voices tell their stories.

In my first book, *Time Among the Navajo: Traditional Lifeways on the Navajo Reservation*, I documented the traditional tasks and activities of the Navajo people. After it was published, Los Angeles photographer David Young-Wolff asked me, "If you write another book on Navajo culture, would you let me take the photographs?" Of course I said yes. Together, David, his wife, Pam, and I undertook the endeavor of creating *Voices of Navajo Mothers and Daughters: Portraits of Beauty*. The couple devoted an incredible amount of energy and time to completing this work. David and Pam made more than twelve trips, each time driving 500 miles from Santa Monica, California, to Flagstaff, Arizona. Then, the three of us traveled to the Navajo Reservation for interviews and photography shoots. Their pictures captured the essence and beauty of Diné women. I believe these images truly honor the connection of mothers and daughters. I cannot thank David and Pam enough for their constant support, enthusiasm, and participation in this project.

It took more than the twenty-one Navajo families for David, Pam, and me to create *Voices of Navajo Mothers and Daughters: Portraits of Beauty*. Many individuals offered their expertise and connections. My husband, Bill, was a tremendous help with the technological aspects of the work and editing. I greatly appreciate his knowledge and skill. Also, I thank him for his tolerance while I worked on this project.

Jim Kieffer, former Superintendent of Sanders Public Schools, located nine families to participate. Jim, who spent a week with us, set up our living quarters and accompanied us to every family interview. Nancy Chaney, Dr. Mark Crane, Jennie Haag, Dr. Rich Haag, Ben Hufford, Elaine Kasch, Sue Kelly, Ann Kramer, Dr. Amy Smith, Mike Tulloss, and Dr. Risha VanderWey provided the contacts and information for mothers and daughters. Kay Ainsworth, Tim Barmettler, Jeneda Benally, Nancy Bené, Dr. Sara Boughner, Nancy Chaney, Dr. Bettie Crane, Ryan Crane, Kathy Furstnow, Russ Furstnow, Megan Hooker, Jan Koons, Marilyn Petersen, Josh Stroup, Linda Stroup, and Darcie Whitney aided in the editing of this work. I value the time they spent on the manuscript.

And finally, I am especially grateful to Julie Hammonds and Myles Schrag of Soulstice Publishing, who realized the importance in this work. Because *Voices of Navajo Mothers and Daughters: Portraits of Beauty* portrays the essence, spirit, and heart of Navajo women, it aligns with Soulstice's philosophy of publishing books with soul. Julie led a team of women to facilitate the creation of *Voices*. Abbie Gripman brought her extensive journalistic experience to the forefront and oversaw the organization of the project. She offered invaluable insight and a positive perspective. Samantha Honanie gave a comprehensive analysis of the many facets of Navajo culture and edited the copy. I thank her for her enthusiasm, in-depth knowledge, and amazing support. Hannah Fontes and Catherine Bell were diligent proofreaders. This team of women welcomed the addition of Corey Begay, who designed the beautiful book you now hold.

To all who helped in creating *Voices of Navajo Mothers and Daughters: Portraits of Beauty*, a documentation of magnificence and culture, I express my deepest gratitude.

Notes

1. Billy Luther, "Letter from the Filmmaker: Miss Navajo," (January 2007), www.ITVS.org/outreach.
2. Raymond Friday Locke, *The Book of the Navajo*, (New York: Kensington Publishing Corp., 2001), 16–17.
3. Victoria Parnell, "Mythological Girls: Changing Woman," (December 29, 2015), www.girlmuseum.org.
4. "Changing Woman: A Navajo Legend," https://www.firstpeople.us/FP-Html-Legends/Changing_Woman-Navajo.html.
5. Joanne McCloskey, *Living Through the Generations: Continuity and Change in Navajo Women's Lives*, (Tucson: The University of Arizona Press, 2007), 17.
6. "Changing Woman: A Navajo Legend," (January 2022), www.firstpeople.us/FP-Html-Legends/Changing_Woman-Navajo.html.
7. *Living Through*, 45.
8. Charlotte Johnson Frisbie, *Kinaaldá, A Study of the Navaho Girl's Puberty Ceremony*, (Salt Lake: University of Utah Press, 1993), 9.
9. Jaclyn Roessel, "Origins of the *kinaaldá*," (October 24, 2012), www.grownupnavajo.com.
10. *Living Through*, 45.
11. *Living Through*, 17, 18.
12. *Living Through*, 50.
13. *Living Through*, 45, 191.
14. Harold Carey, Jr., "The Spanish and the Navajo," (April 15, 2014), www.navajopeople.org.
15. Peter Iverson, *Diné: A History of the Navajos*, (Albuquerque: University of New Mexico Press, 2002), 23.
16. *Diné*, 24, 46.
17. Mads Jakobsen, "The Full History of Navajo Blankets and Rugs," (May 9, 2018), www.heddels.com.
18. *Living Through*, 51.
19. *Diné*, 37–38.
20. *Diné*, 39.
21. Robert Roessel, *Pictorial History of the Navajo From 1860 to 1910*, (Rough Rock: Rough Rock Demonstration School, 1980), 10.
22. *Diné*, 49.
23. *Diné*, 50.
24. *The Book*, 348.
25. *Diné*, 50.
26. Clyde Kluckholm and Dorthea Leighton, *The Navaho*, (Cambridge: Harvard University Press, 1974), 40.
27. *Pictorial*, 11.

28. *Diné*, 55.
29. *Diné*, 52.
30. *Diné*, 51, 55.
31. *Diné*, 51.
32. *The Book*, 364–366.
33. *The Book*, 368.
34. *Diné*, 63–67.
35. *Diné*, 64.
36. Emily Benedek, *The Wind Won't Know Me*, (New York: Alfred Knopf, 1992), 23.
37. *Diné*, 69.
38. *The Wind*, 34.
39. Jeneda Benally, personal communication, February 26, 2022.
40. *The Wind*, 34–35.
41. *Diné*, 73.
42. *The Wind*, 35.
43. *The Wind*, 81, 134.
44. *Diné*, 266.
45. *The Book*, 470.
46. *The Wind*, 33.
47. *The Wind*, 33.
48. *The Wind*, 211–213.
49. *The Book*, 407–408.
50. *Diné*, 82.
51. *Living Through*, 50.
52. *The Book*, 416.
53. *The Book*, 412.
54. *The Book*, 412–413, 417.
55. *Diné*, 115–120.
56. *The Navaho*, 142.
57. *The Navaho*, 142.
58. Alysa Landry, "Assimilation Tool or a Blessing? Inside the Mormon Indian Student Placement Program," (September 13, 2018), www.indiancountrytoday.com.
59. Sacha Pfeiffer, "To Limit COVID-19, Navajo Leader Says: Listen To Your Public Health Professionals," (September 15, 2020), www.npr.org.
60. Frances Stead Sellers, "It's Almost 2020 and 2 Million Americans Still Don't Have Running Water, According to Report," (December 11, 2019), www.washingtonpost.com.
61. Margaret Brennan, "Transcript: Jonathan Nez on Face the Nation," (April 4, 2021), www.cbsnews.com.
62. Creede Newton, "Navajo Nation Outpaces much of US in Delivering COVID Vaccines," (February 9, 2021), www.aljazeera.com.

Bibliography

Benedek, Emily. *The Wind Won't Know Me*. New York: Alfred A. Knopf, 1992.

Bruchac, Joseph. *Navajo Long Walk*. Washington, D.C.: National Geographic Society, 2002.

Frisbie, Charlotte Johnson. *Kinaaldá: A Study of the Navaho Girl's Puberty Ceremony*. Salt Lake City: University of Utah Press, 1993.

Hooker, Kathy Eckles. *Time Among the Navajo: Traditional Lifeways on the Reservation*. Flagstaff: Salina Bookshelf, Inc., 2002.

Iverson, Peter. *Diné: A History of the Navajos*. Albuquerque: University of New Mexico Press, 2002.

Locke, Raymond Friday. *The Book of the Navajo*. New York: Holloway House Classic, 2001.

McCloskey, Joanne. *Living Through the Generations: Continuity and Change in Navajo Women's Lives*. Tucson: University of Arizona Press, 2007.

Mitchell, Rose. *Tall Woman: The Life Story of Rose Mitchell, a Navajo Woman, c. 1874–1977*, ed. Frisbie, Charlotte. Albuquerque: University of New Mexico Press, 2001.

Roessel, Robert, Jr. *Pictorial History of the Navajo from 1860–1910*. Rough Rock, Navajo Nation: Navajo Curriculum Center Rough Rock Demonstration School, 1980.

Scudder, Thayer. *Expected Impacts of Compulsory Relocation on Navajos with Special Emphasis on Relocation from the Former Joint Use Area Required by Public Law 93-531*. New York: Institute for Development Anthropology, Inc., 1979.

Thompson, Hildegard. *The Navajos' Long Walk for Education*. Tsaile: Navajo Community College Press, 1975.

About the Author and Photographer

Kathy Eckles Hooker in Jean Mann's Kitchen

Kathy Eckles Hooker was born in Palo Alto, California, and grew up in a Virginia suburb of Washington, D.C. Her introduction to Native American cultures began as a child watching Native dancers perform at the Department of the Interior. Kathy attended The College of Wooster in Wooster, Ohio, and graduate school at Antioch College in Yellow Springs, Ohio. She and her husband moved to the Navajo Reservation in the 1970s, where he practiced dentistry and she taught English to Diné students at Dilcon Boarding School. Amazed at how the Diné honored and utilized their land, Kathy studied their traditional lifeways and from her research wrote *Time Among the Navajo: Traditional Lifeways on the Reservation*. Later, she taught English at Flagstaff Unified School District for thirty-three years, where again she worked with Diné students. She lives with her husband in Flagstaff, Arizona. The couple has two adult daughters.

Elsie Nez and David Young-Wolff

Light, the real language of photography, communicated the story and path of David Young-Wolff. As a youngster he spent time noticing the way light sashayed between leaves, around mountains, sneaking over and under any object in its way. Being a photographer, he utilized the language of light to reveal what was important in each of his photographs.

During nearly forty-four years as a professional photographer in Los Angeles, he became one of the top producers of stock photography. He moved from stock photography to a niche shooting yoga, fashion photography, and creative portraiture. He captured evocative images for his clients and at the same time worked on personal photography projects.

He considers his collaboration on *Voices of Navajo Mothers and Daughters: Portraits of Beauty* with author Kathy Hooker to be one of the highlights of his career. He met many people and heard stories about Navajo life. The experience, he said, was an incredible education and a privilege. David and his wife, Pam, now live near Bend, Oregon, where he continues to follow the light.

We dedicate this book to our daughters and son: Megan, Sara, Kelly, and Colin.

Voices of Navajo Mothers and Daughters: Portraits of Beauty

ISBN: 978-1-7349899-2-2
Library of Congress Control Number: 2022901888
Graphic design by Corey Begay
Composed in Mr Eaves XL Mod OT
Editorial services by Abbie Gripman, Julie Hammonds, and Samantha Honanie
Printed in Canada by Friesens

Soulstice Publishing
PO Box 791
Flagstaff, AZ 86002
(928) 814-8943
connect@soulsticepublishing.com
www.soulsticepublishing.com
9 8 7 6 5 4 3 2

About the Publisher

Soulstice Publishing brings to life "books with soul" that inspire readers with stories of human potential realized and celebrate our unique position in the Southwest.

Soulstice took root in our mountain town of Flagstaff, Arizona, which sits at the base of the San Francisco Peaks, on homelands sacred to Native Americans throughout the region. We honor their past, present, and future generations, as well as their original and ongoing care for the lands we also hold dear.

Surrounded by ponderosa pines, enriched by diverse cultures, and inspired by the optimistic Western spirit, Flagstaff abounds with scientists, artists, athletes, and many other people who love the outdoors. It is quite an inspiring place to live. Considering the dearth of oxygen at our 7,000-foot elevation, you might say it leaves us breathless.